WE COULD
THE SONGWRITING ARTISTRY OF

Boudleaux + Felice Bryant

COUNTRY MUSIC FOUNDATION PRESS

222 FIFTH AVENUE SOUTH · NASHVILLE, TENNESSEE 37203

Published 2019. Printed in the United States of America.

978-0-915608-33-1

This publication was created by the staff of the Country Music Hall of Fame® and Museum.

Editor: Jay Orr · Artifact photos by Bob Delevante · Printer: Lithographics, Inc., Nashville, Tennessee

PRESENTED BY

Willard&Pat Walker
Charitable Foundation, Inc.

Boudleaux and Felice Bryant, 1980s

2

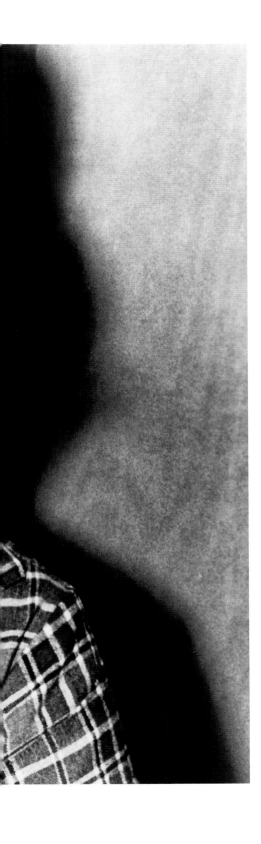

CONTENTS

ACKNOWLEDGMENTS

The Country Music Hall of Fame® and Museum would like to thank Del and Dane Bryant, the sons of Boudleaux and Felice, for their generous donation of their parents' vast collection, which includes the Bryants' songwriting ledgers, musical instruments, business documents, photographs, recordings, personal correspondence, and much more.

We are also grateful to the Willard and Pat Walker Charitable Foundation. In addition to sponsoring the exhibit, the Walker Foundation is helping to preserve the Bryant Collection and make it accessible to researchers through a generous partnership with the museum.

Ms. Lee Wilson deserves special thanks for her research in annotating *All I Have to Do Is Dream: The Boudleaux and Felice Bryant Story*, a box set produced by House of Bryant Publications in 2011. This set features numerous family photos, three CDs (two comprising covers of Bryants songs, one of demo recordings), and a DVD documentary of the Bryants' lives and work. Ms. Wilson's insightful annotations were published in book form by Nashville's Two Creeks Press, 2017.

Jeri Hasty, of House of Bryant, and Marc Wood, Sr., of Sony/ATV Music Publishing Nashville, were essential in providing examples of motion pictures, television programs, and commercials that have used Bryant songs. Also deserving of our thanks for providing images and items that were vital to telling this story are Margaret Everly, Jim Lauderdale, and Roy's Boys, LLC.

As always, we thank the Metropolitan Nashville Arts Commission and the Tennessee Arts Commission for their continued support of museum programs and exhibitions.

Many museum staff members devoted time and talent to the book and the exhibit. Space prohibits listing them all, but a few deserve mention here. Vice President of Museum Services Brenda Colladay and Executive Director of Exhibition Services John Reed led the curatorial team, which consisted of John Rumble, Mick Buck, Alan Stoker, Shepherd Alligood, Bryan Jones, Elizabeth Edwards, Juli Thanki, and Senior Registrar Elek Horvath. Editor Jay Orr, Senior Creative Director Warren Denney, Creative Design Manager Bret Pelizzari, Associate Creative Director Jeff Stamper, Associate Director of Quality Control Chris Richards, Graphic Designer Chad Steinborn, and Senior Production Manager Debbie Sanders deserve special recognition.

OPPOSITE PAGE:
Del, Dane, Felice, and Boudleaux Bryant, c. 1970

Boudleaux Bryant at home, 1970s
Photo: Bing T. Gee

DEAR MUSEUM PATRON,

Anywhere else, it would have been a fountain. But this was Milwaukee, Wisconsin, where water fountains are called "bubblers." This was the Hotel Schroeder, a short walk from Lake Michigan, and the bubbler allowed one of American popular music's most fortuitous meetings.

In the spring of 1945, Georgia-reared musician Boudleaux Bryant was playing jazz in the Schroeder's cocktail lounge. Matilda Genevieve Scaduto was operating the elevator near the bubbler where Boudleaux sought refreshment. They met, conversed, launched a whirlwind romance, and ran off together within the week.

Their running off was somewhat scandalous, especially to glowering family members, but their settling down enriched all of us. Matilda soon took the name of Felice, and Felice became Boudleaux's lifelong creative partner. Without the bubbler communion, we would not have "Love Hurts," "Bye Bye Love," "Wake Up Little Susie," "Rocky Top," "Country Boy," "Sleepless Nights," "Like Strangers," or thousands of other gems.

Together, they wrote more than 6,000 songs that sold many millions of records. Their compositions were recorded by Eddy Arnold, Ray Charles, Buddy Holly, Emmylou Harris, Bobbie Gentry, Bob Dylan, Simon & Garfunkel, Norah Jones, Roy Orbison, the Osborne Brothers, and, especially, the Everly Brothers. The Bryants became Nashville's first professional songwriters. And they became members of the Country Music Hall of Fame. "We were the factory," Felice told Lydia Hutchinson of *Performing Songwriter* magazine. The factory produced melody, harmony, elevated lyricism, and good food. Recording artists would visit the Bryants' house, gorge on Felice's Italian delicacies, and then sit in satisfied pasta comas while Boudleaux played them songs. The Bryants' was a home of love and creativity, where legends convened and conversed, and where partnerships were conceived.

The Bryants wrote down their songs in ledgers, and those ledgers are now—thanks to the visionary generosity of sons Dane and Del Bryant—in the safe and steadfast custody of the Country Music Hall of Fame and Museum. We keep these treasures secure, and we ensure that they will be available to edify generations of learners, scholars, and seekers.

Nashville boasts a sculpture called *Musica* at the roundabout that serves as the entrance to Music Row, the place where so many songs are created, recorded, and marketed. In 2019, Nashville leaders determined that the sculpture should be augmented by fountains that signify the font of creativity. And so plans are underway for the Boudleaux and Felice Bryant Fountains of *Musica*. That's probably because the "Boudleaux and Felice Bryant Bubblers of *Musica*" doesn't sound right, south of Wisconsin.

Kyle Young | CEO

7

Boudleaux and Felice Bryant, late 1970s

One Heart, One Spirit, One Purpose

By Thom Schuyler

Thom Schuyler moved to Nashville in 1978 to pursue a career in songwriting. During his forty years on Music Row, more than two hundred of his songs were recorded, including fifteen Top Ten hits. He was elected to the Nashville Songwriters Hall of Fame in 2011.

Songs and songwriters fascinated me at an early age. From the Methodist hymns of Fanny Crosby to the folksongs of the 1950s to the collaborations of composers and lyricists for Broadway productions to the diverse offerings to be heard on Top Forty radio in the 1960s—all filled me with awe and admiration. For me, the most edifying credits on any 45 rpm disc or LP appeared in parentheses beneath the song titles: the names of the songs' composers.

So, when I arrived in Nashville, in 1978, I knew very well the names Boudleaux and Felice Bryant. They were living legends, held in high regard by so many who flocked to Nashville to attempt to do what the Bryants had done. Within a few years of my arrival—thanks to the kindness of their son Del—I met the couple and found them to be warm and welcoming, down to earth and full of life. And, of course, I was star struck.

It has been stated, fairly and accurately, that Boudleaux and Felice Bryant were the first two people to move to Nashville for the sole purpose of making a living in the city by writing songs. Popular recordings had been created in Nashville by stars of the Grand Ole Opry, including DeFord Bailey; by Francis Craig and His Orchestra; and by Eddy Arnold. Prior to the Bryants' arrival in 1950, a majority of the songs that got recorded were composed in other musical centers such as New York, Chicago, and Memphis. The Bryants' relocation to Nashville marked a significant milestone in the evolution of what had been a sleepy, Southern town, into globally celebrated Music City, USA; and, perhaps more importantly, the Bryants' arrival shone like a beacon to thousands of musicians and poets longing to find a community of like-minded dreamers, determined to pursue a career in songwriting. In the ensuing seventy years, countless men and women have

From left: Country Music Hall of Fame members Felice Bryant, Dolly Parton, and BMI executive Frances Preston, 1970s

followed the path marked by Boudleaux and Felice Bryant in the 1950s. Few, however, have achieved the success of this remarkably talented couple. The Bryants' creative spirit, dedication to their craft, pursuit of excellence, and astonishing catalog of hit songs ushered in the Era of the Songwriter in Nashville, Tennessee—the Town Where the Song Is King.

Many readers of this book and visitors to this exhibit will not have heard of Boudleaux and Felice Bryant. For the most part, songwriters work in (and mostly enjoy) anonymity within the music industry. Seeking out the identity of a composer on an old vinyl recording, or in CD liner notes that are becoming increasingly rare, or in mp3 files (where liner notes typically don't exist) is a practice reserved for the most voracious music lover. Recording artists typically get all the public recognition. To a certain degree Boudleaux and Felice changed even this part of the songwriters' landscape. As their work flourished in the 1950s and 1960s, a bit of their anonymity began to peel away, and their celebrity increased. One factor in that development was their important role as suppliers of songs that launched the careers of the legendary Everly Brothers. Readers unfamiliar with the Bryants' names will surely know the Bryant-written songs that became major hits by Phil and Don Everly: "Bye Bye Love," "Wake

Up Little Susie," and "All I Have to Do Is Dream." These widely popular records also helped alter the perception of Nashville as strictly a country music center, and they inspired what eventually became an exodus of the most talented musicians, singers, and songwriters from across the globe to Middle Tennessee—a trend that continues to this day.

Matilda Scaduto met Boudleaux Bryant in 1945 in her hometown of Milwaukee, Wisconsin, where she was an elevator operator at the Hotel Schroeder, and he a traveling musician. They were married quickly and soon settled down in Boudleaux's hometown—Moultrie, Georgia. Boudleaux was so enchanted by his new bride he began calling her Felice—a term of deep affection that means *Happiness*. While Boudleaux continued working in various traveling bands, Felice—a bit lonely and bored—began writing poems and song lyrics. When Felice shared some of her words with Boudleaux, he began structuring chord progressions and melodies to accompany her words and in short order they had compiled a catalog of eighty songs. Early attempts to garner the attention of music publishers in New York finally resulted in an opportunity to move to Nashville as writers and songpluggers for Tannen Music.

Following this relocation to Nashville, and over the course of their decades-long career, the Bryants composed over six thousand songs (an unimaginable output) of which nine

hundred were recorded (another astonishing number). Included in that repertoire (along with the aforementioned Everlys hits) are the classics "Love Hurts," "We Could," "Devoted to You," "Take a Message to Mary," "Rocky Top" (performed at every ceremony and sporting event at the University of Tennessee, Knoxville), and many more. This abridged list of their masterful work resulted in their induction into the Nashville Songwriters Hall of Fame, the Songwriters Hall of Fame, the Country Music Hall of Fame, and the Rockabilly Hall of Fame. Further, what must not be lost in this narrative is the diverse array of artists—representing multiple musical genres—that recorded the Bryants' songs: Little Jimmy Dickens, Carl Smith, the Osborne Brothers, Gram Parsons, Emmylou Harris, Simon & Garfunkel, the Beach Boys, Ray Charles, and Bob Dylan are but a few.

It is difficult to imagine that Nashville, Tennessee, would have become the musical mecca it became without the unparalleled influence of Boudleaux and Felice Bryant. Indeed, scores of talented folks followed them and composed masterpieces, but would they have made the trip and commitment without the Bryants' example and success? They blazed a beautiful trail, and the road was more welcoming and hopeful because of their talent and perseverance.

On the occasion of their passing—Boudleaux in 1987 and Felice in 2003—I was asked by their devoted sons, Del

and Dane, to deliver their eulogies—a singular honor. As I was preparing remarks for Felice's service I realized I had said so much about both of them at Boudleaux's funeral. Then the reason became very clear: Boudleaux and Felice shared one heart, one spirit, and one purpose; more than anything theirs was a remarkable Love Story, and we all benefited from the joy and zest for life they found with one another. Another thing became clear: There were many more individuals far more articulate than I, and with the help of Del, I was able to collect and include the following quotes at the end of Felice's eulogy:

Boudleaux Bryant and Willie Nelson, c. 1963

The first time I was ever moved enough to seek out the name of a songwriter was on an Everly Brothers recording of a Felice and Boudleaux Bryant song. They were my favorite writers and a powerful early influence. —Paul Simon

The songs Felice Bryant wrote with her husband Boudleaux have given untold pleasure to the world, and her lyrics must have inspired hundreds of songwriters and singers. All those classics remain a pleasure and an inspiration, as fresh today as they were when they were created. —Mark Knopfler

Boudleaux and Felice Bryant's work had a tremendous influence on me, especially early in my career when I modeled my best efforts on the lovely, elegant songs they penned for the Everlys. Their contribution to the country/pop genre is immeasurable and irreplaceable. —Jimmy Webb

I am one of the millions who have been deeply moved by the simple and elegant poetry of Felice Bryant. Quiet and constant, she has been a light to those of us who have dreamed we could do what she has done to express in her easy and open way what is deep in our hearts. —James Taylor

They were the kind of people you can call up just to say "Hello," and they believed you. —Jack Clement

The most beautiful picture that anyone could see was to be around Felice and Boudleaux. They were in love and it showed. We will all miss them. —Eddy Arnold

Happiness!

Thom Schuyler – Jekyll Island, Georgia – August 2019

Felice Bryant, Minnie Pearl, and an unidentified woman clowning around at a golf tournament, 1970s. *Photo: Joe Rudis for the* Nashville Tennessean

WE COULD
THE SONGWRITING ARTISTRY OF

Boudleaux + Felice Bryant

By John Rumble

Boudleaux and Felice Bryant fused their steadfast work ethic with a sly command of melody, meter, and concise, cinematic lyricism to become prolific and noteworthy contributors to the Great American Songbook. Over their long career, doing business from Nashville, the couple composed more than six thousand songs, and around nine hundred of them were recorded by country, pop, and R&B artists, many of whom enjoyed worldwide audiences. The Bryants' stylistically diverse offerings ranged from "Country Boy," their first hit, in 1949, recorded by "Little" Jimmy Dickens; to the pop standard "Have a Good Time," recorded by Tony Bennett, Billy Eckstine, and Ruth Brown; to the bluegrass classic "Rocky Top." Nashville's first full-time professional songwriters, they set an influential example by establishing their own publishing companies. This exhibit celebrates not only their musical achievements, but also their remarkable personal love story.

AN UNLIKELY PAIR

In many ways, Boudleaux and Felice Bryant were an unlikely pair. Born in 1920 in Shellman, Georgia, Diadorius Boudleaux Bryant was the son of Louise Parham and small-town lawyer Daniel Bryant. Named for a French soldier who saved Daniel's life during World War I, Boudleaux grew up in Moultrie, Georgia, in a Protestant family that included three boys and two girls. Felice, of Sicilian and French descent, was born Matilda Genevieve Scaduto in 1925 to Milwaukee barber Salvatore "Sam" Scaduto and Katherine Loverdi. Felice and her sister, Kitty, were raised in the Catholic Church. Boudleaux was

handsome, calm, and six feet, two inches tall. Felice—attractive, outspoken, and fiery—stood just over five feet, one inch. Yet both loved music. Boudleaux studied classical violin from age five and learned hoedowns from his father and from fiddlers Daniel brought home for supper. Boudleaux also toured widely with the Bryants' family band, which traveled as far as Texas and Chicago. Like the Bryants, Felice's extended clan played various instruments, and though she played none, she loved to sing, read, and write poetry. In addition, she appeared on local radio as a child and acted in stage productions during her teens.

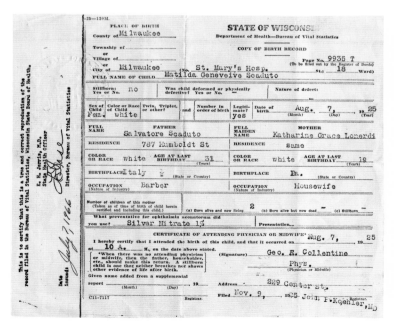

Felice Bryant's birth certificate

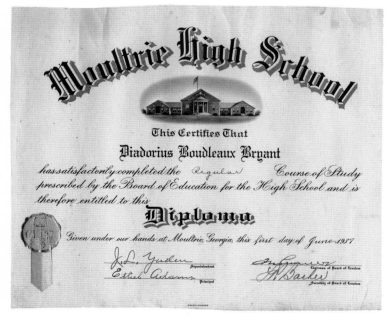

Boudleaux Bryant's high school diploma

Boudleaux Bryant, 1921

Felice Bryant's father, Salvatore Scaduto, holds her older sister, Kitty, and baby Felice in this family portrait, c. 1925.

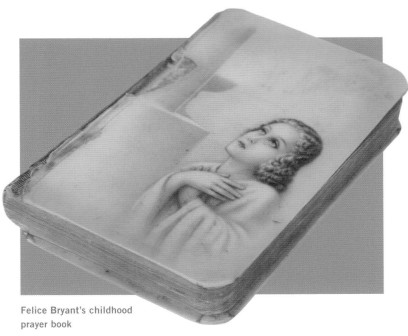

Felice Bryant's childhood prayer book

YOUNG MAN WITH A FIDDLE

After finishing high school in Moultrie in 1937, Boudleaux played violin with the Atlanta Philharmonic Orchestra for the 1937–1938 season. But performing with Gene "Uncle Ned" Stripling and His Texas Wranglers, the young musician found that he could make more money with string band music than he could with selections from the classics. From 1938 into the early 1940s, he worked radio shows and tours with various Atlanta-based country groups, including Stripling's band and Hank Penny's Radio Cowboys, a western swing outfit in which Bryant played hot, jazzy fiddle. Fifty-thousand-watt WSB, Atlanta's premier radio enterprise, featured country series such as the *Cross Roads Follies*, *Pop Eckler's Radio Jamboree*, and the *WSB Barn Dance*. The station's far-reaching signal made it possible for acts from these programs to book shows at schoolhouses and theaters and play radio engagements throughout the Southeast. "We ranged from the Gulf Coast as far north as Norfolk," Boudleaux said.

During a 1940 trip to Chicago with Penny, Bryant first recorded an original instrumental, "Tobacco State Swing," for the Columbia subsidiary OKeh Records. In Atlanta, Doug Spivey and Marvin Taylor, billed as the Pine Ridge Boys, recorded Bryant's "No Matter What Happens"

Boudleaux Bryant, late 1930s
OPPOSITE PAGE: **Boudleaux Bryant used this violin throughout his career.**

Certificate of Person Performing Marriage Ceremony

TO BE DELIVERED TO PARTIES MARRIED

No. _____

I, _Rev. Paul E. Eninger_ a _minister_

of the _C. G. M._ Church, or religious order of that name,

do certify that on the _5th_ day of _September_ 194_5_

at _Covington_ Kentucky, under authority

of a license issued by GEO. J. KAUFMANN, Clerk of County Court of Campbell County, State of Kentucky,

dated the _5th_ day of _September_ 194_5_, I united

D. Boudleaux Bryant and _Matilda G. Scaduto_

Husband and his Wife, in the presence of _E Gilbert_ and _Lela Eninger_

Given under my hand, this _5th_ day of _September_ 194_5_

Rev. Paul E. Eninger

PERSON PERFORMING CEREMONY—SIGN HERE

Minister of Religion

TITLE OF OFFICE

HESKAMP PRINT

Marriage certificate for Boudleaux and Felice Bryant

(including both music and lyrics) for RCA's Bluebird imprint in 1941. These recordings barely hinted at his future productivity, but they were a start.

The early forties found Bryant on the road, where he performed hillbilly music over Memphis radio station WMC; played pop tunes in Washington, D.C., supper clubs; and appeared at the Palmer House Hotel in Chicago and special engagements in Detroit, where the Ford Motor Company staged parties whose guests would do square dances on horseback. Wherever he worked, Bryant said,

"We'd play whatever they wanted to hear." When money got tight, he returned to Moultrie, where radio spots and local dances let him earn enough to travel again.

Along the way, Bryant acquired a serious drinking habit. According to his sons, when Boudleaux was seventeen he suffered from stage fright, and a doctor advised him to have a shot of whiskey to help him relax before each performance. Before long, the shot had become a pint, and by the mid-1940s Bryant was waking up with severe hangovers. "It was during this time that Felice and I met,"

Hank Penny and his Radio Cowboys, c. 1940. From left: Louis Dumont, Sheldon Bennett, Noel Boggs, Carl Stewart, Boudleaux Bryant, and Hank Penny.

he said, "and up to that time I must say that I was just gallivanting around the country, having a hell of a good time part of the time, starving part of the time . . . with no sense of direction or anything—just playing and goofing off." Felice helped him control his drinking and gave him a new sense of purpose. Said Chet Atkins, "She kept him away from booze. That was one of her great contributions. And she also brought him the confidence that he could [be a full-time songwriter]."

At age sixteen, Felice had impulsively married a sailor whose military service took them to Texas. She quickly realized her mistake and came home to Milwaukee. Despite the fact that she was still married to her first husband, she and Boudleaux ran off together. Shocked, Felice's mother dragged her home with strict orders not to see Boudleaux until her first marriage was dissolved. Nevertheless, the young lovers communicated by phone and coded written messages. Felice's divorce finalized, the couple wed in Covington, Kentucky, on September 5, 1945.

Boudleaux Bryant joined the Chicago Federation of Musicians in December 1944.

23

Felice and Boudleaux at a nightclub, 1945

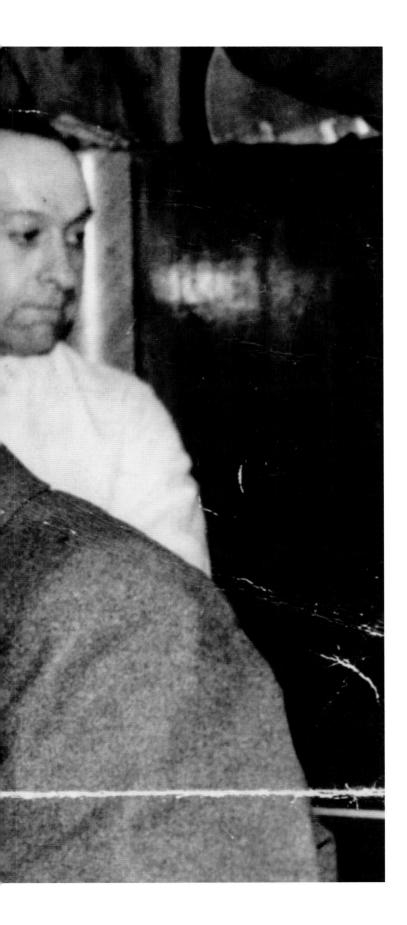

LOVE AT FIRST SPLASH

Felice Bryant met her husband in 1945 at the Hotel Schroeder, in Milwaukee, Wisconsin. "I was an elevator starter," she said. "Boudleaux was a musician at the cocktail lounge at the Schroeder." As an eight-year-old, Felice had dreamed of her future husband. "I was dancing with this gorgeous fellow—big, tall, six-foot-two guy with a beard." When Boudleaux came out of the lounge on a break, she recognized him, even though he was clean-shaven. "I was afraid he'd get away, so I went over to the water fountain, turned on the thing and said, 'Can I buy you a drink?' And that water arced and messed up his tuxedo. That same evening, he introduced me as his fiancée . . . It was love at first splash."

As a young man, Boudleaux had consulted a fortune teller who told him he would marry a woman five years his junior, and that they would become rich. He proposed almost immediately, asking Matilda Scaduto to change her first name to Felice—to reflect her upbeat personality—and her last name to Bryant. "They fell in love from the minute they saw each other," the Bryants' son Dane said. "I think that the pheromones that went off between those two people bound them together tremendously." Dane's younger brother, Del, agreed: "They were madly in love, and that love made everything work."

The Bryants, 1946

Boudleaux kept this double-sided photo of Felice in his wallet for most of his life.

Boudleaux Bryant, La Crosse, Wisconsin, 1942

Felice Bryant, c. 1943

Boudleaux and Felice Bryant performing on their morning program, *Coffee Klatch,* at Green Bay, Wisconsin, radio station WBAY, 1949

Boudleaux and
Felice Bryant, c. 1945

SONGWRITING PARTNERS

"Boudleaux would see my scrap papers around, so he knew I was writing. And then he decided to get in on it with me, and we had so much fun that he couldn't wait to get home at night to see what the heck we were gonna come up with . . . It went both ways. Sometimes I inserted a bridge. Sometimes he took the theme. I'd be humming something around the house and he'd say, 'Honey, is that yours?' I'd say, 'No, no; I heard that on the radio.' Or 'Yeah, that's mine.' And he'd grab it."

– FELICE BRYANT

A Strategic Alliance

In the late 1940s, the Bryants worked together playing music mainly in the Midwest. Following Boudleaux's pattern, they returned periodically to Moultrie, where he played gigs and Felice wrote poems. Soon they started collaborating for their own enjoyment, and after accumulating eighty songs, they began mailing them to publishers they identified in music trade magazines—though they met with little success. During this time, they welcomed two sons: Dane, born in 1947, and Del, who followed in 1948. In Cincinnati, when Del was "in the chute" (as Felice said), the Bryants showed their song "Country Boy" to singer Rome Johnson, Boudleaux's former musical partner in Detroit. Johnson immediately called Nashville music publisher Fred Rose, his MGM Records producer. Johnson introduced Boudleaux to Rose on the telephone, and sent Rose a recorded demo of the song. Rose did not think the number fit the smooth-singing Johnson and placed it instead with rising Grand Ole Opry star "Little" Jimmy Dickens, who made it a #7 country hit for Columbia in 1949.

Del (in bassinet) and Dane Bryant outside the Bryants' house trailer in Moultrie, Georgia, 1949

Sheet music, published 1948

The Bryant family at their home on Old Hickory
Lake, Hendersonville, Tennessee, c. 1958

Family portrait, early 1950s. From left: Del, Boudleaux, Felice, and Dane Bryant.
Photo: Olan Mills

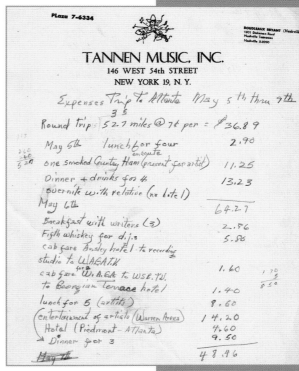

During one of the Bryants' visits to Moultrie, Rose sent the cash-strapped Boudleaux seventy-five dollars so he could bring more material to Nashville; Rose also accepted several more songs for publication. Famed for writing pop hits such as "Deed I Do" and top-sellers for cowboy star Gene Autry, Rose became the Bryants' mentor. With his help, Boudleaux became a salaried songplugger for New York publisher Nat Tannen, with the understanding that Boudleaux would only pitch Bryant material and let Rose have any songs he wanted for pop singers. Bryant hits would soon enrich the catalog of Acuff-Rose Publications, the music publishing company Rose had formed with Grand Ole Opry headliner Roy Acuff in 1942.

TOP RIGHT: Boudleaux Bryant listed his travel expenses while working as a songplugger for Nat Tannen. BOTTOM RIGHT: In this 1949 letter to Boudleaux Bryant, Fred Rose expressed his interest in publishing "Country Boy."

Nashville's Music Scene

At Rose's urging, the Bryants moved to Nashville in 1950. "We were poor enough that we had to take it in stages," Boudleaux said. "We came to Macon, Georgia, and I got a job with a little dance outfit. We stayed there for about a month until we could get enough money to buy gas and come on up to Nashville." Felice did her part as well: "The band was so poor that they needed a girl singer [to work] for nothing. I said, 'Here I am.'"

The struggling couple settled in a Dickerson Road trailer park just as Nashville's music industry was taking off. Prior to World War II, radio station WSM had helped to make the Tennessee capital a vital broadcasting center. In 1932, the station boosted its signal strength to fifty thousand watts, providing wider exposure that enabled radio talent to make distant personal appearances with help from WSM's booking department and local agents. Since 1942, Acuff-Rose had risen to national prominence with country and pop hits such as "Tennessee Waltz" and "Chattanoogie Shoe Shine Boy," both million sellers released in 1950. WSM executive Jack Stapp founded Tree Music in 1951, and Jim Denny, also a WSM manager, organized Cedarwood Music in 1953. Although the Victor Talking Machine Company (later RCA Victor) recorded several Opry performers in Nashville in 1928, local commercial recording had languished during the Great Depression. As World War II revived the U.S. economy, RCA signed handsome, mellow-voiced Eddy Arnold in 1943; in December 1944, he recorded Nashville's first modern-day session, acting as his own producer and using a WSM studio. Through 1949, RCA producer Steve Sholes held most of Arnold's sessions in Chicago or New York. Paul Cohen, Sholes's counterpart at Decca Records, led the way in recording in Nashville, where Opry stalwarts Ernest Tubb, Red Foley, and later, Kitty Wells had easy access to the Castle Recording Laboratory, a groundbreaking enterprise launched by WSM engineers shortly after World War II ended.

During the postwar decade, as the Grand Ole Opry's weekly half-hour NBC network segment grew to more than 170 stations, WSM recruited many of country music's leading artists. Combined with Nashville's central location, broader radio exposure multiplied opportunities for songwriters, music publishers, talent agents, and record companies, including major labels and local startups such as Bullet Records.

LEFT: Jimmy Sweeney recording session at Owen Bradley's Nashville studio, c. 1958. From left: Hank Garland, Lightnin' Chance, Jimmy Sweeney, Boudleaux Bryant, and Floyd Cramer. Sweeney recorded Boudleaux and Felice Bryant's "She Wears My Ring" in 1960. *Photo: Elmer Williams*

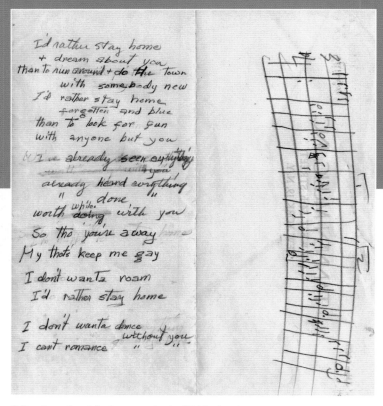

Felice Bryant's original manuscript for "I'd Rather Stay Home."
Kitty Wells had a hit with her recording of the song in 1956.

Kitty Wells, 1955. *Photo: Elmer Williams*

In 1950, the year the Bryants arrived, ace guitarist and future RCA producer Chet Atkins returned to WSM from Springfield, Missouri, and WSM announcer David Cobb aptly coined the moniker "Music City, U.S.A." while introducing Red Foley's featured NBC network radio show.

The Bryants became fixtures backstage at the Opry. Boudleaux made the most of the access by finding out which artists needed songs. "And Boudleaux never said no," Felice said. If Boudleaux had nothing, he and Felice would tailor new songs to fit each artist's needs.

He often invited performers home, where they could enjoy Felice's Italian cooking, look through the Bryants' songwriting ledgers, and hear them demonstrate their material firsthand.

Early on, Opry stars Jimmy Dickens and Carl Smith recorded several Bryant songs. Dickens pleased fans with "I'm Little but I'm Loud" in 1950 and had a hit with "Out Behind the Barn" in 1954. During 1952 and 1953, Smith found success with "It's a Lovely, Lovely World" and the chart-topping "Hey, Joe!" Fred Rose pitched "Hey, Joe!" to Columbia producer Mitch Miller, who recorded it with

Western wear designer Nathan Turk made this suit, with arrowhead stitching, for Carl Smith.

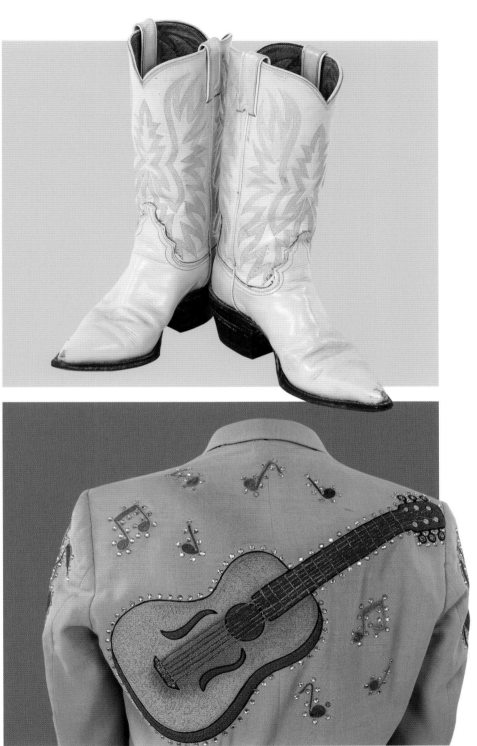

Little Jimmy Dickens performed in these Justin boots (top) and this jacket from Nudie's Rodeo Tailors, embellished with rhinestones and embroidery.

pop sensation Frankie Laine. The Bryants promoted Laine's version to East Coast disc jockeys, and in 1953 it went #11 pop. Columbia pop star Tony Bennett had a Top Twenty pop hit with "Have a Good Time" in 1952. Jazz singer Billy Eckstine and R&B queen Ruth Brown each recorded a version of this song, which was one of the Bryants' most reliable moneymakers. In 1953, Red Foley—then headlining the Opry's NBC segment—topped the country chart with "Midnight," a song written by Boudleaux and Chet Atkins.

BELOW: The Bryants used this Wollensak tape recorder, built in the 1950s, to record song ideas and home demos.

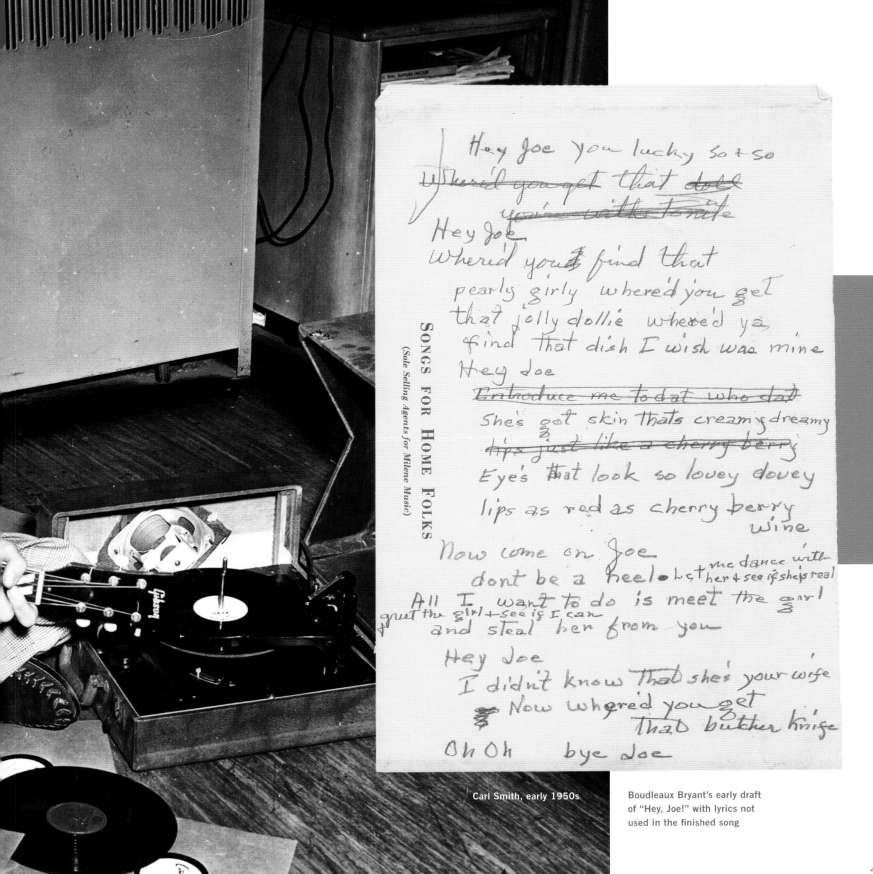

SONGS FOR HOME FOLKS

(Sole Selling Agents for Milene Music)

Hey Joe you lucky so + so
~~Where'd you get that doll~~
~~you~~ ~~with Fonzie~~
Hey ~~Joe~~
Where'd you ~~t~~ find that
pearly girly where'd you get
that jolly dollie where'd ya
find that dish I wish was mine
Hey Joe
~~Entroduce me to dat who dat~~
She's got skin thats creamy dreamy
~~lips just like a cherry berry~~
Eye's ~~that~~ that look so lovey dovey
lips as red as cherry berry
                              wine

Now come on Joe   me dance with
     dont be a heel let her + see if she's real
All I want to do is meet the girl
greet the girl + see if I can
     and steal her from you

    Hey Joe
    I didn't know That she's your wife
    ₰ Now where'd you get
                    that butcher knife
Oh Oh   bye Joe

Carl Smith, early 1950s

Boudleaux Bryant's early draft
of "Hey, Joe!" with lyrics not
used in the finished song

41

Pasta Scam

Nashville's close-knit community of music industry professionals often mixed business with leisure. The Bryants used their home as a creative workshop and business office, and they wrote most of their songs there. The couple also pitched their songs at home. They would often invite performers to come for a dinner of Felice's Italian cuisine. "They were not well traveled," Felice observed. "The country field was quite innocent." As she cooked spaghetti or other Italian favorites, artists would relax and savor the pleasant aromas coming from the kitchen. Their guests at ease, Boudleaux would show them new songs. Felice might add harmony, sing a backing vocal, or suggest a lyric, all in the interest of selling the song. "I fed them until they couldn't move," she recalled of the ritual they called their "pasta scam." "Boudleaux would have a captive audience," she said. "They had to listen, and to get out, they had to take something. We'd trap 'em!"

ABOVE: Felice Bryant in her kitchen, c. 1960

BELOW: Boudleaux Bryant at home, c. 1959, pitching a song to the Omegas (from left: Bill Fernez, Earl Sinks, and Norro Wilson). The Omegas recorded several of the Bryants' songs.

PASTA SAUCE
à la Felice Bryant

For 1 Pound Spaghetti

Basic Tomato Sauce with Ground Meat

ingredients {
¼ cup olive oil or salad oil
4 medium onions chopped
1 or 2 pounds chopped meat
2 6 ounce cans of tomato paste
1 number 2 can of tomatoes (strained)
6 cups of water
Salt + pepper to taste
Teaspoon of sugar
}

Step 1   Heat oil in large enamel or stainless steel saucepan

"   2   Brown onions in oil 'til soft & golden

'   ~~Add tomato paste, tomatoes and water~~

"   3   Add chopped meat — cook slightly 'til gray

"   4   Add tomato paste, tomatoes and water

"   5   Stir 'til well blended

"   6   Add seasonings

"   7   Simmer uncovered til sauce is thick (rolling boil will burn sauce — Soft bubbles are necessary to thicken sauce)

Felice Bryant's recipe for pasta sauce

Felice Bryant wrote messages to Boudleaux on the inside front covers of their song ledgers. *Photo: Elmer Williams*

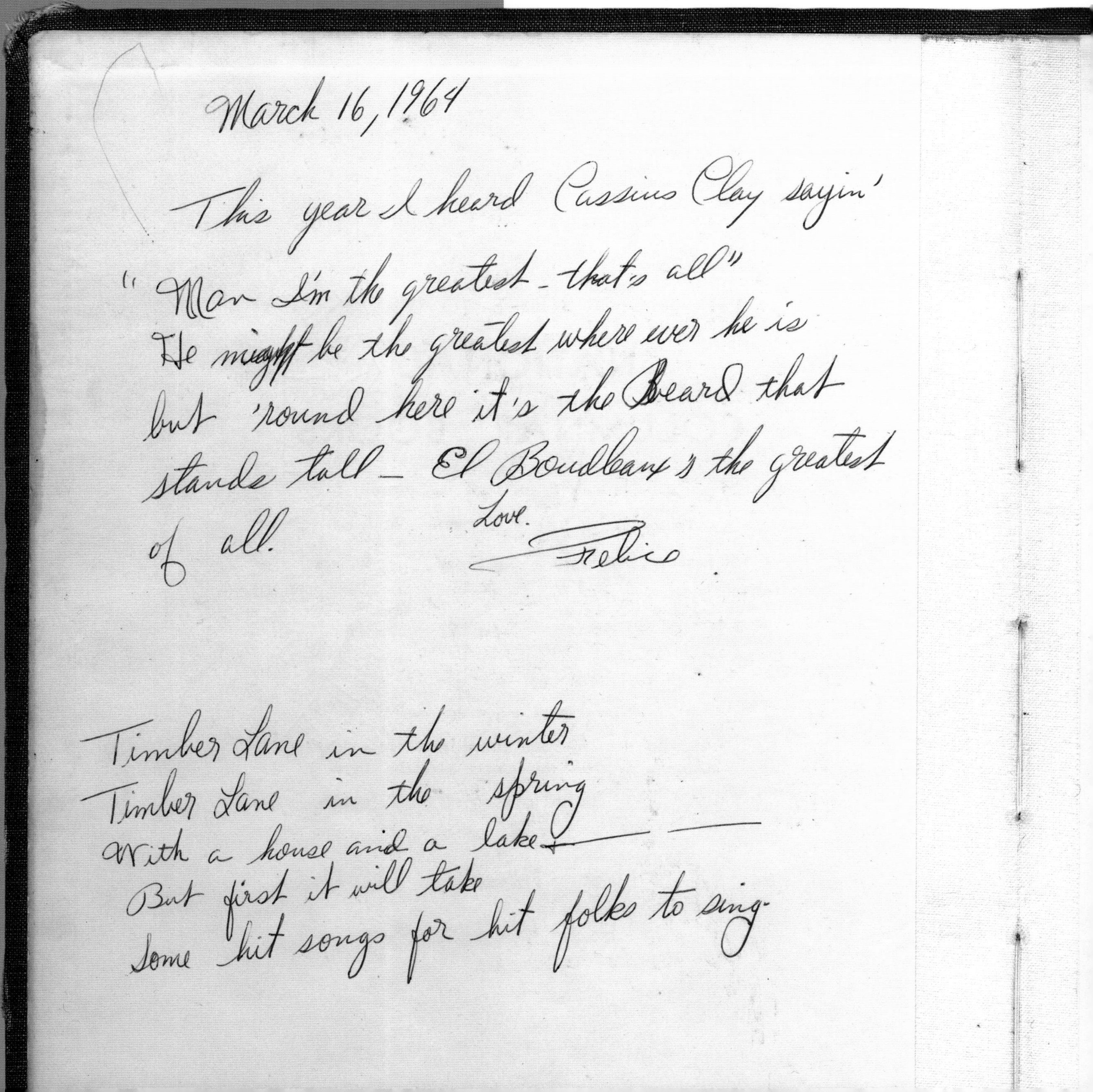

March 16, 1964

This year I heard Cassius Clay sayin'
"Man I'm the greatest - that's all"
He might be the greatest where ever he is
but 'round here it's the Beard that
stands tall — El Boudleaux's the greatest
of all.

Love.
Felice

Timber Lane in the winter
Timber Lane in the spring
With a house and a lake!
But first it will take
Some hit songs for hit folks to sing.

Boudleaux and Felice Bryant, c. 1960. *Photo: Elmer Williams*

BEGINNINGS AND ENDINGS

Although the Bryants got many of their Tannen Music songs recorded, they were eager to control their own publishing rights, and in 1954 they left Tannen to form Showcase Music. Within two years, the Bryants counted some forty commercial recordings of songs in their catalog, among them Bobby Lord's rendition of "Hawk-Eye"; "The Richest Man (in the World)," a #10

Fred Rose. *Photo: Walden S. Fabry Studios*

The Bryants looking at a photo of singer Bobby Lord, c. 1955. Lord recorded several of the Bryants' songs.
Photo: Elmer Williams

Bobby Lord autographed this promotional photo "Mom," his nickname for Felice Bryant.

Manuscript for "Hawk-Eye"

country hit for Eddy Arnold; and "We Could," a Jimmy Dickens favorite that Felice wrote for Boudleaux as a birthday present.

On December 1, 1954, the Bryants lost Fred Rose, their chief advisor and advocate, whose songwriting gifts, knack for matching songs and artists, and widespread contacts in the music industry nurtured their career. By the time a heart attack ended Rose's life, he had helped the Bryants establish themselves as songwriters. "We survived because we had faith and Fred Rose," Felice affirmed. For the rest of their lives, the Bryants gave Rose's photo a place of honor in their home.

47

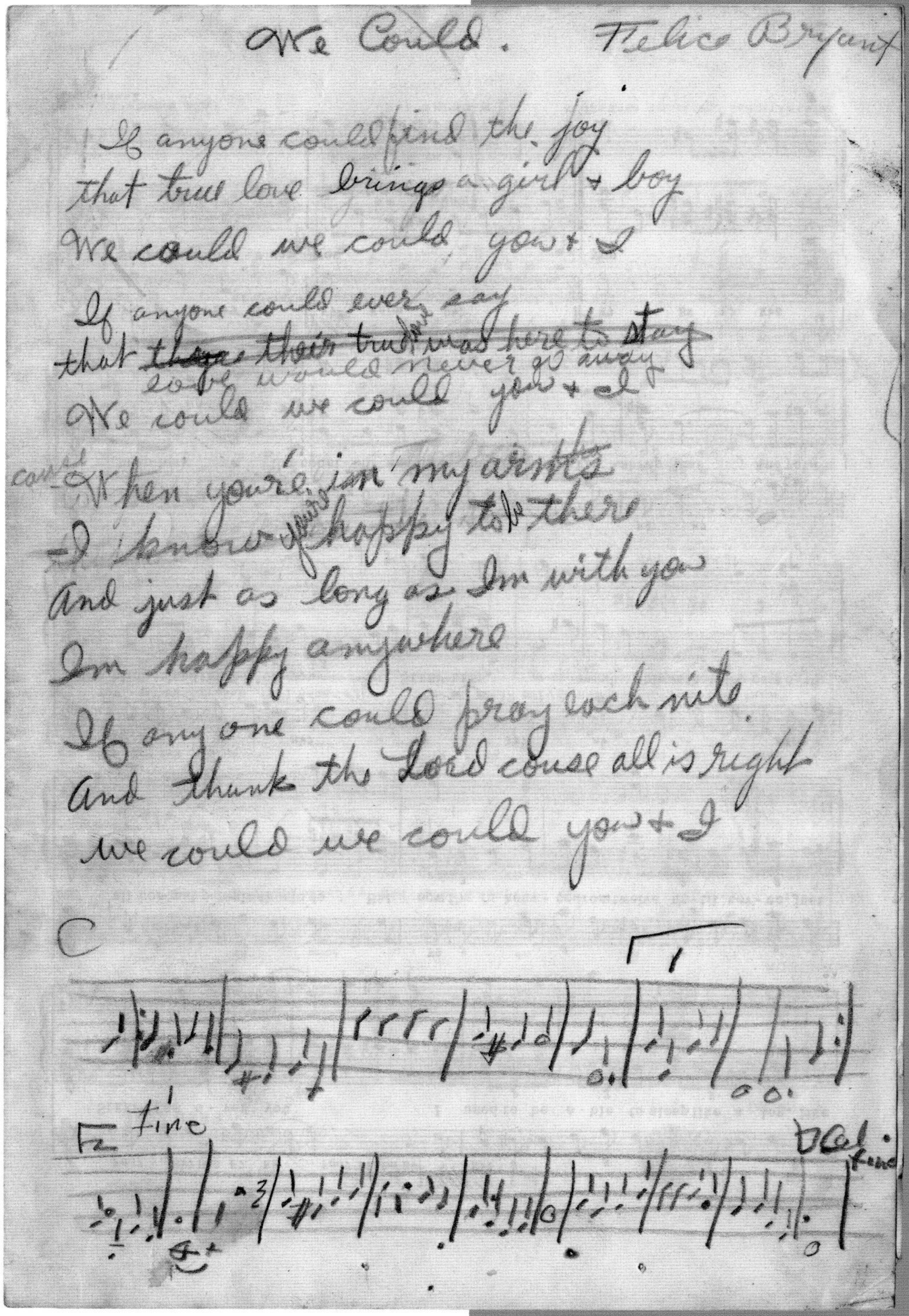

Felice Bryant's manuscript for "We Could"

"We Could"

"It was a birthday present to my husband, Boudleaux . . .
He was laying on the couch; he likes to lay on the couch
when he's working. I was sitting in the chair directly
across from him and he fell asleep. I kept looking at him
and thinking, 'How precious,' and I thought, 'If anybody
could make this old world whistle, we could, we could.'
If you want to talk about inspirational tunes, that song
came so fast it was all I could do to write it down. My
name's on it, but it was there so fast, I don't even feel like
I wrote it."

– Felice Bryant

(Feb 13, 1956) Belated birthday gift— March 23, 1956

To the biggest baby in the family
& the best pal, a pal ever had.
I'll love you forever, and longer
if you want me to

Felice

Chet Atkins and Boudleaux Bryant, 1971

Outside the Acuff-Rose Studio, c. 1960
From left: Lester Rose, Boudleaux Bryant,
Wesley Rose, and Bud Brown

Boudleaux and Felice Bryant with Wesley Rose
at his Acuff-Rose Publications office, c. 1960

A PIONEERING BUSINESS DEAL

The Bryants had left Nat Tannen because he declined their offer to write exclusively for his company if Tannen agreed to return copyrights on their songs after ten years. Fred Rose had also passed on this proposal, advising the Bryants that Acuff-Rose would not be able to handle the large number of songs he predicted they would generate. For this same reason, Rose returned any of their songs he could not get recorded. Rose had made his son Wesley general manager of Acuff-Rose in 1945, and in late 1956, Wesley gave the Bryants the deal they were seeking. Having lost Hank Williams in 1953 and his father the following year, Wesley needed to sign writers of the Bryants' caliber to maintain—and even increase—the company's prominent place in American music. "I think Boudleaux and Felice Bryant are two of the most talented songwriters that I have ever heard," he said in 1984. "Because many times I would say to Boudleaux, 'How about going on home and write me a song for X?' Now, there's many great writers in town, but they're not able to aim." The Bryants wanted to write full-time, and they knew that Acuff-Rose aggressively promoted its catalog in various media and across genres. In return for the reversion of their publishing rights after a decade, the Bryants agreed to write strictly for Acuff-Rose and lease the valuable Showcase catalog to the company for this same period. One of the first of its kind in Nashville, the shrewd deal made good sense, and almost immediately yielded spectacular results.

Recording session for singer Bob Luman at Nashville's RCA recording studio, c. 1960. From left: RCA engineer Bill Porter, Wesley Rose, Warner Bros. president James Conkling, and Boudleaux Bryant. *Photo: Elmer Williams*

A Very Simple Little Thing

"A song is a very simple little thing, if you come right down to it. It is an idea that's reduced to just a very few words and not very many notes, and it's got to be something that strikes the ear and is memorable to you, at least for a little while, and something that you want to hear again. That part doesn't change about songs."

– Boudleaux Bryant

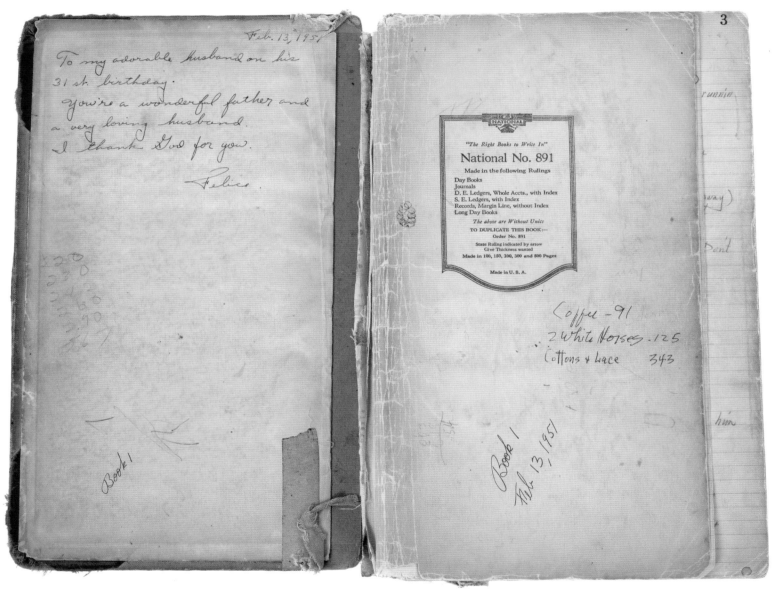

Feb. 13, 1951

To my adorable husband on his
31 st. birthday.
  You're a wonderful father and
a very loving husband.
I thank God for you.
               Felice

Book 1

"The Right Books to Write In"

National No. 891

Made in the following Rulings

Day Books
Journals
D. E. Ledgers, Whole Accts., with Index
S. E. Ledgers, with Index
Records, Margin Line, without Index
Long Day Books

The above are Without Units

TO DUPLICATE THIS BOOK:—
Order No. 891
State Ruling indicated by arrow
Give Thickness wanted
Made in 100, 150, 200, 300 and 500 Pages

Made in U. S. A.

Coffee - 91
2 White Horses - 125
Cottons & Lace   343

Book 1
Feb 13, 1951

The first of sixteen accounting ledgers in which the
Bryants wrote their songs. Felice inscribed a birthday
message to Boudleaux on the inside cover.

Felice and Boudleaux Bryant at their
home in Gatlinburg, Tennessee, mid-1980s

Now At Last---You Can Find The RIGHT WORD At A Glance!

SISSON'S SYNONYMS

An Unabridged Synonym and Related Term Locater

by A.F. SISSON

Thesaurus, book of synonyms, and rhyming dictionary used by the Bryants while writing songs

Felice and Boudleaux with sons Dane (left) and Del in their Hendersonville High School marching band uniforms, mid-1960s

SONGWRITING, BRYANT-STYLE

"Mom was a compulsive writer; she *had* to write. Our father was impressed with the money he could make writing. And he had the talent . . . I know that Mom saw Dad as the craftsman and the finisher . . . and Mom would *start* 'em lots of times. She wrote in yellow pads, and I know that she would get an idea—start off on a verse or get the melody and a little verse, and then she would give that to Dad."

– DANE BRYANT

"Dad was more cerebral. Dad was writing all the time. He was thinking about his melodies all the time . . . and you didn't necessarily know to what extent he was working on songs just watching him . . . Mother, you *knew* what she was doing because it was all coming out of her mouth. She was walking around singing . . . Dad would go, 'What was that, Felice? Do that again' . . . and then he'd start with something and start crafting it and give it a toe or a foot or a leg, and then they'd start working from *that* . . . He would write it all down in the ledger. And he'd be writing it down during the process a lot."

– DEL BRYANT

HITMAKERS:
THE BRYANTS AND THE EVERLY BROTHERS

In 1957, Wesley Rose signed Don and Phil Everly as Acuff-Rose songwriters and brokered their recording contract with Cadence Records. The first Bryant song the Everlys accepted was "Bye Bye Love," previously rejected by thirty different acts. Recorded at RCA's McGavock Street studio in Nashville, the Everlys' catchy performance combined high-pitched sibling harmony, rock & roll rhythms, and the simple, direct story of a broken romance. It was the duo's first hit; in 1957 it reached #1 on *Billboard*'s country chart while rising to #2 on its pop chart and #5

on the publication's R&B chart. Next, the Everlys took the Bryants' "Wake Up Little Susie"—recorded at the same studio—to #1 on all three charts. Network TV appearances, and a national rock & roll tour with acts such as Chuck Berry and Fats Domino, sent the brothers' record sales skyward and extended their radio airplay. In 1958 and 1959, they had continued success in country and pop with Bryant classics such as "All I Have to Do Is Dream," "Bird Dog," and "Devoted to You," all recorded at the Nashville studio on 17th Avenue South later known as

From left: Phil Everly, Wesley Rose, Boudleaux Bryant, and Don Everly, backstage at the Grand Ole Opry, late 1950s. *Photo: Elmer Williams*

94

H.O.B.

Bye Bye Love
Felice and Boudleaux Bryant

Bye Bye Love Bye Bye happiness
Hello loneliness
I think I'm gonna cry
Bye Bye love
Sweet caress
Hello emptiness
I feel like I could die
Bye Bye my love Bye Bye

[musical notation]

sweetheart
There goes my baby with someone new
She sure looks happy I sure am blue
I thought she loved me she didn't care

She was my baby Til he stepped in
Goodbye to romance that might have been

[musical notation]

free from
I'm through with romance I'm through with love
" " " countin' the stars above
+ here's the reason that I'm so free
My lovin' baby is through with me

206

Wake Up Little Susie   Boudleaux Bryant
                                        Felice Bryant

little
Wake up Susie   Wake up
Wake up Susie   " "

We've both been sound asleep
weep   Wake up little susie and weep
heap   The movies over It's four oclock
leap   And we're in trouble deep
            Wake up little Susie
Susie open up your eyes
Your in for a big surprise

[musical notation]

[musical notation]

What are we gonna tell your mama
"   "   "   gonna   "   our pa
When they say Ooh la la

Wake Up Susie

Cut by Everly Bros.
Boudleaux Bryant
Joe Melson
A.R. 10   R & B record – Merc. 1967
         Riverboat Soul Band Merc, 196
Simon & Garfunkel 1952 (W. Bros.)

Original manuscripts for "Bye Bye Love" and "Wake Up Little Susie"

MASTERS AND STUDENTS

"Their stuff fit us like a glove, because it was designed to fit. Boudleaux would sit down and talk with us. A lot of his songs were written because he was getting inside our heads—trying to find out where we were going, what we wanted, what words were right."

– DON EVERLY

"They were masters. Anybody would be a fool not to watch how they did it. That's the level that you wanted to be at. I learned more from them than from anybody."

– PHIL EVERLY

Made in Mexico, these Faosa sunglasses were worn by Roy Orbison in the 1960s.

Don and Phil Everly, c. 1960

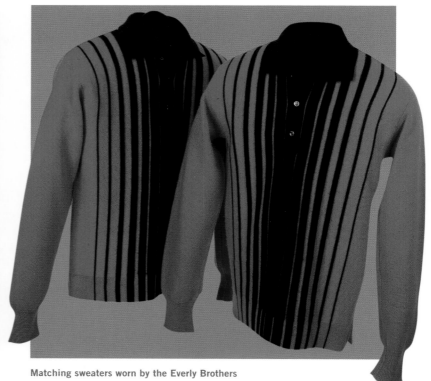

Matching sweaters worn by the Everly Brothers

RCA Studio B. Once the Everlys' career ignited, the Bryants faced stiff competition from other writers and music publishers. "Our material did get preference," Boudleaux said. "But it had to stand the test." It passed with flying colors. All told, the Everlys recorded twenty-nine Bryant songs, with some selling millions worldwide. Those hits helped make the Everlys and the Bryants rich and world-famous, filled Acuff-Rose's coffers, heightened Studio B's visibility, and expanded Nashville's reputation as a diverse music center. Moreover, Chet Atkins said, the Bryant–Everly alliance gave Boudleaux and Felice tremendous international impact: "Many of their songs, recorded by the Everly Brothers, greatly influenced the Beatles, who, in turn, influenced the whole world of music."

Boudleaux and Felice Bryant helped the Everly Brothers create hits that led to a lucrative ten-year recording contract. As the act's manager, Wesley Rose negotiated this pact with Warner Bros. in 1960, and the Everlys' original "Cathy's Clown," one of the first singles they recorded for the label, eventually sold eight million copies. But in 1961, the Everlys fired Rose as their manager when he tried to force them to record Acuff-Rose company songs only, a move that disrupted the schedule of Everly releases.

TOP: Boudleaux Bryant and Roy Orbison, mid-1960s
BOTTOM: Original manuscript for "Love Hurts"

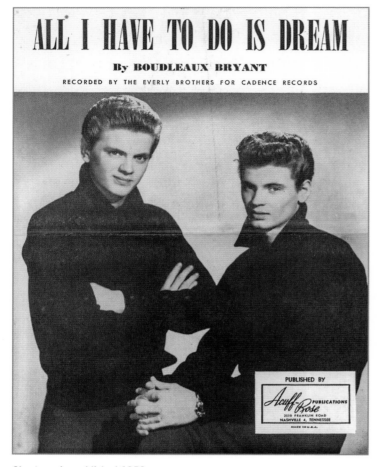

Sheet music, published 1958

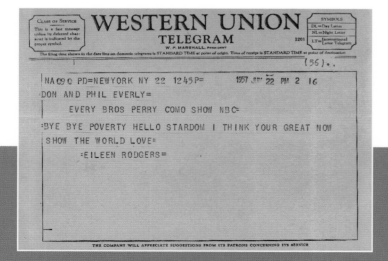

In retaliation for his dismissal, Rose blocked the Everlys' access to new Bryant songs. The Everlys had country and pop hits into the early 1960s, but the Bryant–Everly team was sidelined.

The Bryants might have sued Rose for damages, yet they took the long view. The publishing rights on all their songs written between 1957 and 1967, including those recorded by Don and Phil Everly, began reverting to the Bryants in 1967, at the end of each song's ten-year term. The songs had plenty of life left in them, and they continued to be recorded by top singers. In the meantime, they kept connecting with singers such as rockabilly stylist Bob Luman, whose version of "Let's Think About Living" was a million-selling country and pop hit of 1960. In 1961, Bob Moore and His Orchestra went #7 pop with Boudleaux's instrumental "Mexico." Earlier Bryant material also found new interpreters in RCA's Jim Reeves, whose velvet voice was perfect for "We Could" (1960), and Ray Charles, who selected "Midnight" for his album *Modern Sounds in Country and Western Music, Volume Two* (ABC, 1962). Both Sue Thompson and Roy Hamilton released versions of "Have a Good Time" in 1962 and 1964, respectively.

LEFT: The Everly Brothers performed "Bye Bye Love" on their debut appearance on NBC-TV's *The Perry Como Show*, June 22, 1957. They received this telegram from a fan.

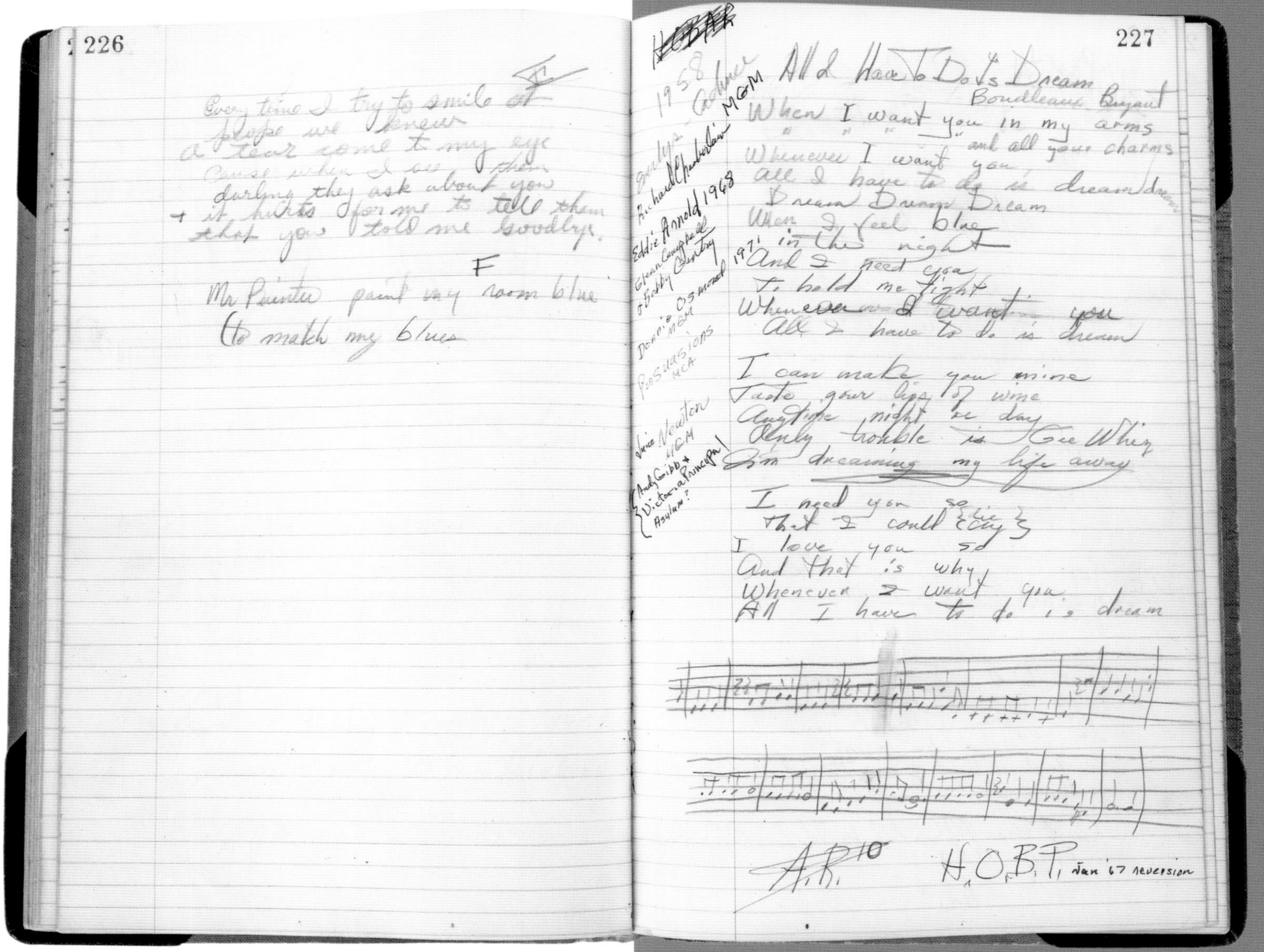

Every time I try to smile at
people we knew
a tear come to my eye
Cause when I see them
darling they ask about you
+ it hurts for me to tell them
that you told me Goodbye.

F

Mr Painter paint my room blue
(to match my blues

H.O.B.T

1958
Everly's Cadence MGM
" " Richard Chamberlain
Eddie Arnold 1963
Glenn Campbell
& Bobby Gentry
Donnie Osmond
MGM
Personations
MCA

June Newton
MGM
Andy Gibb +
Victoria Principal
Asylum?

All I Have To Do Is Dream
Boudleaux Bryant

When I want you in my arms
" " " " and all your charms
Whenever I want you,
all I have to do is dream dr
Dream Dream Dream
When I feel blue
1971 in the night
And I need you
to hold me tight
Whenever I want you
All I have to do is dream

I can make you mine
Taste your lips of wine
Anytime night or day
Only trouble is Gee Whiz
I'm dreaming my life away

I need you so
that I could die
I love you so
And that is why
Whenever I want you,
All I have to do is dream

A.D.10 H.O.B.T. Jan '67 reversion

Original manuscript of "All I Have to Do Is Dream"

The Bryants in London, early 1980s

Masters of Harmony

"The harmony is something that Boudleaux has always been able to do because of his violin training . . . So when the Everlys came along, they fell in love with the material that Chet Atkins fell in love with way before the Everlys showed up . . . But we needed the Everlys and evidently the Everlys needed us and we met. So I don't know who made who, but I tell you, we all had a good time."

– Felice Bryant

The Bryants in the 1970s
Photo: Bing T. Gee

06264
TAKE A MESSAGE TO MARY

Words and Music by
FELICE BRYANT and
BOUDLEAUX BRYANT

Recorded by
BOB DYLAN
on Columbia Records

HOUSE OF BRYANT PUBLICATIONS   90¢

Sheet music, published 1970

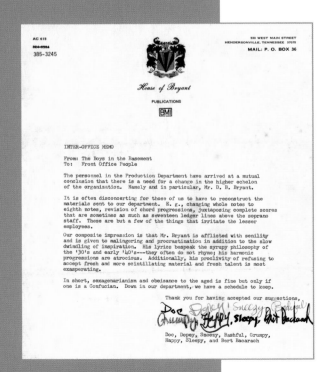

**Satirical memo on House
of Bryant stationery**

HOUSE OF BRYANT

In 1967, Boudleaux and Felice Bryant began reclaiming the U.S. copyrights for songs they had written since 1957 for Acuff-Rose. The ten-year reversions had been called for in the Bryants' contract with the company. International publishing rights remained with Acuff-Rose, and the Bryants continued to receive the writers' share of foreign royalties. As the copyrights came back to Boudleaux and Felice, the couple moved the songs into their House of Bryant publishing company, where the songs continued to see impressive activity. The high quality of the Bryants' work made Acuff-Rose an attractive acquisition for larger companies. Opryland Music Group bought the company in 1985, and was, in turn, acquired by Sony in 2002.

Bob Dylan, producer Bob Johnston, and singer Dolores
Edgin at Nashville's Columbia Studio A, 1969

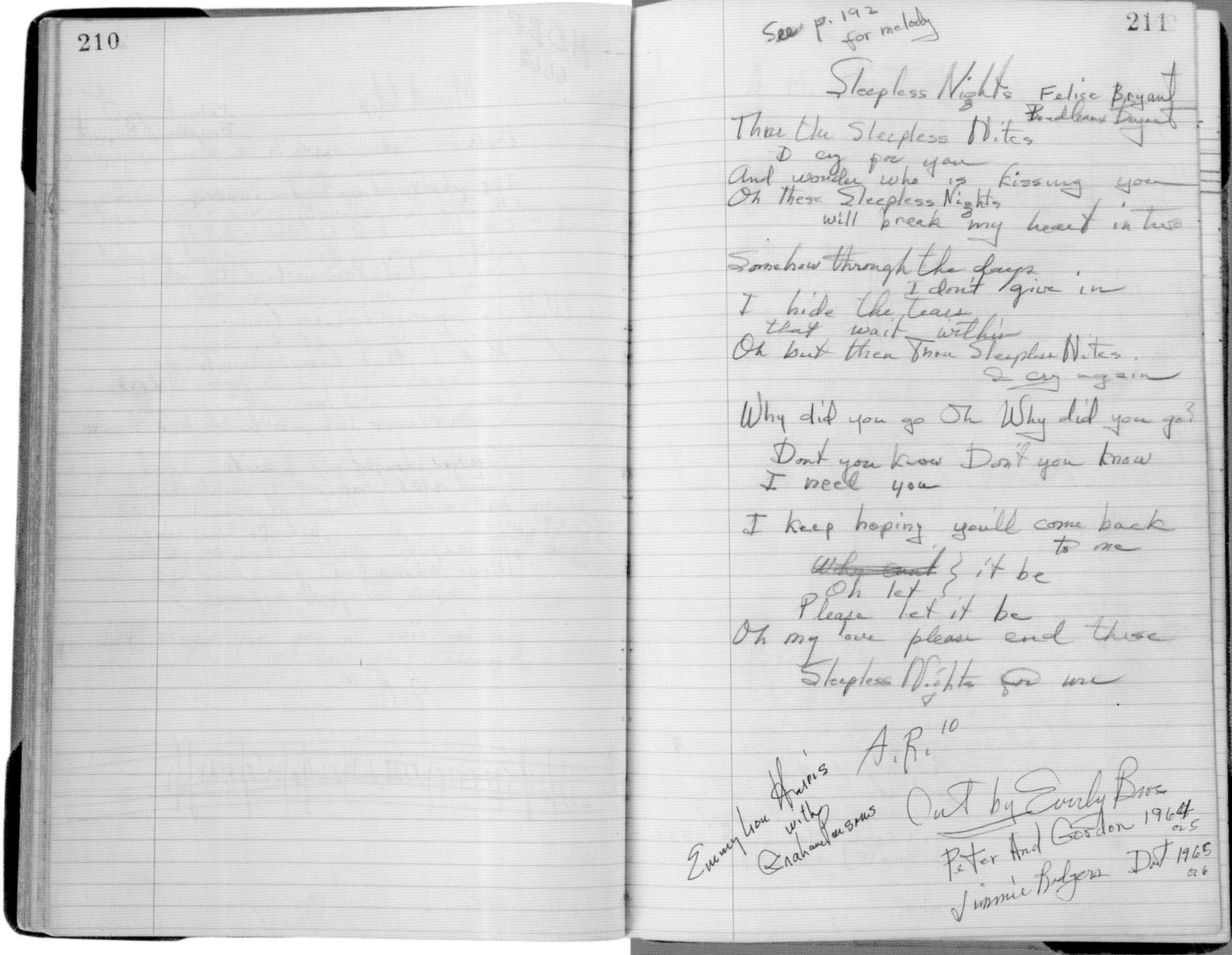

210

211

See p. 192 for melody

Sleepless Nights Felice Bryant
                  Boudleaux Bryant

Thru the Sleepless Nites
    I cry for you
And wonder who is kissing you
Oh these Sleepless Nights
        will break my heart in two

Somehow through the days
            I dont give in
I hide the tears
    that wait within
Oh but then Thru Sleepless Nites.
            I cry again

Why did you go Oh Why did you go?
    Dont you know Dont you know
    I need you

I keep hoping you'll come back
                    to me
Why cant } it be
    Oh let }
    Please let it be
Oh my love please end these
    Sleepless Nights for me

A.R. 10

Emmylou Harris
    with
Graham Parsons

Out by Everly Bros 1964
Peter And Gordon   025
Jimmie Rodgers DJ 1965
                    026

The Bryants' original manuscript of "Sleepless Nights"

The Bryants, 1970s
Photo: Bing T. Gee

ROCKY TOP

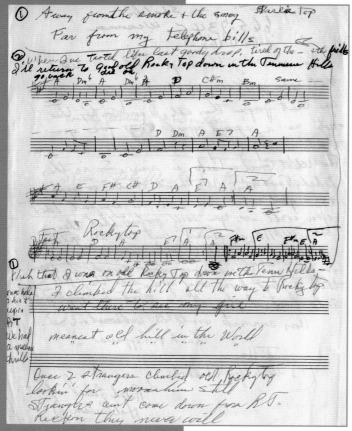

TOP: **Governor Lamar Alexander congratulates the Bryants on "Rocky Top" being named a Tennessee state song, 1982.**

BOTTOM: **Early draft of "Rocky Top"**

The Bryants grew House of Bryant with new hits as well. Among them was "Rocky Top," one of the world's most popular bluegrass songs. In August 1967, Boudleaux and Felice booked a motel room in Gatlinburg, Tennessee, to work on sentimental songs for country star Archie Campbell, then planning an album titled *The Golden Years*. Days of continuous writing passed, and Felice grew tired of culling out negative aspects of aging, obviously inappropriate for the project. As Boudleaux recalled, "She put her foot down and said, 'We've got to write something else,' and I didn't really want to, but after a little bit of an argument I said, 'Well how's *this*?' and started off into 'Rocky Top.' She said 'That's great!' and she fell in. [We] just started doing the melody and the words—the whole thing came together, all at one time. It just happened; it just fell into our basket and there it was."

Back in Nashville, bluegrass artist Sonny Osborne called, asking if they had any songs for an upcoming album he was planning to record with his brother, Bobby. "Well, Sonny comes over and Boudleaux plays it," Felice said. "And [before Boudleaux finishes singing] Sonny says, 'That's fine; that's fine.'" The Osborne Brothers recorded "Rocky Top" later that year. Their rendition reached #33 on the country charts in 1968, and dozens of other artists—including Lynn Anderson, Dolly Parton, Porter Wagoner, Buck Owens, and Dinah Shore—made the song a standard.

The Bryants accept the thanks of fans at the University of Tennessee's Neyland Stadium, September 23, 1978.

"Rocky Top" became one of Tennessee's official state songs in 1982 and it remains a favorite at University of Tennessee sports events. For bluegrass bands everywhere, "Rocky Top" is still an essential crowd-pleaser. An injury forced Sonny Osborne to retire from music, but at this writing Bobby still leads his band, the Rocky Top X-Press. "If I'm at the Opry and I have two songs [to play], one of them will be 'Rocky Top,'" he said. "And if I just do one song in the segment, that one will be 'Rocky Top.'" Osborne has performed it thousands of times, not only at the Grand Ole Opry but also at bluegrass festivals and symphony halls in the U.S. and overseas. "It's the greatest feeling there ever was," he said. "I never dreamed in my whole lifetime that I'd ever be a part of something like that."

ABOVE: The University of Tennessee's Pride of the Southland Band salutes the Bryants, early 2000s. RIGHT: The band performs "Rocky Top" during a halftime tribute to the Bryants at Knoxville's Neyland Stadium, September 23, 1978.

Rocky Top Village Inn, Gatlinburg, Tennessee

OSBORNE BROTHERS
Grand Ole Opry

Boudleaux Bryant
used this 1961
Martin 0-16NY to
write "Rocky Top."

ABOVE: The Osborne Brothers made the first recording of "Rocky Top,"
in 1967. The bluegrass stalwarts also recorded the Bryants' "Tennessee
Hound Dog" (1969) and "Georgia Pineywoods" (1971). From left:
Bobby Osborne, Dale Sledd, Sonny Osborne, and Ronnie Reno.

81

Cut Smith Columbia   1st Record Osbourne Bros (open sales)

Gary Paxton MGM   F#m E G A G D A E A   Album by Lynn Anderson

Rocky Top

Boudleaux & Felice Bryant

F#m Fast   F#m E F#m E D.C.

Cho.   F#m E G A G D A E A   Cut for Album by Bill Anderson Decca   Single by Dinah Shore   Porter Wagoner RCA   Decca — released May 69   Conninly twitty Decca   Lynn Anderson Chart

Cut by Dillard + Clark A+M , Chet Atkins, RCA. , Boosey Reed RCA, Jimmy Dean RCA, Boots Randolph Monument, Roy Clark Dot, Buck Owens Capitol, Charley McCoy Mon, Danny Davis, Victor, Everly Bros, Victor , Sweeny MGM.

Wish that I was on old Rocky Top
    down in the Tennessee hills

Had some good old times on Rocky Top

Ain't no smoggy smoke on Rocky Top
" " telephone bills

Once I had a girl on Rocky Top
I still dream about that
half-tame mountain pussy cat | Half bear - half pussycat |
She was sweet as store bought soda pop
Wild as a mink but sweet as
I still dream about that

Once two strangers climbed old Rocky Top
Lookin for a moonshine still
Strangers ain't come down from Rocky Top
Reckon they never will

The corn don't wont grow at all   too tall
Old Thin Soil is to blame   hardly grow on Rocky Top
But if youre cravin corn on Rocky Top
It's Chile all the same

    soils too rocky by far
That's why the all in a jar
    all the corn in Rocky Top
    Get their corn from a jar

Sold total I spun googoo by Aug. 1973

I've had years of cramped-up city life
Trapped & stomped &   hemmed in
   Trapped like pigs in a pen   ducks
All I know is it's a pity life
can't be simple again

F#m   You'll always be
Rocky Top   You will always be   And
Good   Youre   Home Sweet Home to me
Old Rocky Top Gee I love you
Rocky Top Tennessee
A   G   A

She could dance a strong hog bogganes
   never need a powder
Never even huff or puff
And still have strength to knock his noggin off
If she was not in the mood
you got a little too fast
he   fresh
    quick
If he got a little too rough

Rec. by Osbourne Bros. Decca
Released Jan. 1968 —
Cut Nov 1968 by Dinah Shore - Decca   K.H. Wells Decca

Original manuscript of "Rocky Top"

A Song Is Born

"We spent days working on music, and we were ripe for 'Rocky Top' when it showed up . . . We'd been working for three solid weeks, hard. So we were in fertile territory. Songs were just coming."

– Felice Bryant

"We'd been doing some material for Archie Campbell, for an album he was doing called *The Golden Years*. We were in Gatlinburg in the midst of all that beautiful scenery in the mountains and everything. Felice was really getting tired of *The Golden Years* . . . She said 'I've got to do something else. We've just got to write something happier!' . . . And I didn't really want to, but after a little bit of an argument I said, 'Well how's *this*?' and started off into 'Rocky Top.' She said 'That's great!' and she fell in. We just started doing the melody and the words—the whole thing came together, all at one time. It just happened; it just fell into our basket and there it was."

– Boudleaux Bryant

GATLINBURG

After renovating an old home in Gatlinburg, the Bryants moved there in 1980. Soon they purchased a cluster of motels and renamed it the Rocky Top Village Inn. They still wrote songs and worked on stage musicals, but now they took more time to relax, read, and enjoy each other's company. They also took pleasure in their sons' accomplishments. Dane and Del had grown up in the music industry, watching their parents show songs to a

From left: Dane, Boudleaux, Felice, and Del Bryant in New York, 1986, for Boudleaux and Felice's induction into the Songwriters Hall of Fame

Felice and Boudleaux Bryant at their home in Gatlinburg, Tennessee, early 1980s

parade of acts who came first to the Bryants' trailer, then to a basement house financed with royalty advances from Fred Rose and Nat Tannen, and finally to a beautiful home the couple built on Old Hickory Lake outside of Nashville. Both Dane and Del worked for House of Bryant at various points, recording demos, calling disc jockeys, and pitching songs to producers and artists. Dane started his own publishing company in 1974, formed a second one in the 1980s, and later sold them to Tree Music. Del signed on with performing rights organization BMI's Nashville office in 1972, and after filling many positions within the company, he became President and CEO in 2004. He retired in 2014.

Boudleaux Bryant died in Gatlinburg in 1987. Felice lived there until her death, in 2003.

LEFT: The Bryants' house in Gatlinburg

The key to Room 388 at the Gatlinburg Inn, the Bryants' mountain retreat where they wrote "Rocky Top" and many other songs

The Bryants at their Rocky Top Village Inn, Gatlinburg, Tennessee, 1980s

Felice and Boudleaux Bryant, late 1970s

A Lasting Legacy

As Nashville's first full-time professional writers, Boudleaux and Felice Bryant set high standards for many creative talents who have followed them. "They showed that you can make a living as songwriters," Phil Everly said. "They also showed that you had to go to work at it and be a professional at it . . . You have to write a quality song." Likewise, the Bryants were among the first Nashville songwriters to organize their own publishing companies, inspiring others to do the same. Del Bryant added this perspective in 2011: "I think their lasting influence is, simply put, the songs. Not what those songs mean, or meant, to the artists, but what those songs mean to the culture. They pulled about half a dozen to ten songs out of the ether that everybody still knows today, whether you're eighty years old, or whether you're a young music lover in your teens. You know 'Bye Bye Love,' you know 'All I Have to Do Is Dream,' you probably know 'Rocky Top,' [and] you probably know 'Love Hurts.'" New artists have continued to find new audiences with Bryant originals. Wesley Rose, whose publishing empire the Bryants did so much to enlarge, expressed their ongoing contribution in 1984: "I think the Bryants are writers for all times."

RIGHT: Tuxedo worn by Boudleaux Bryant
OPPOSITE PAGE: The Bryants, mid-1980s

Chet Atkins with the Bryants, 1985

"Felice and Boudleaux Bryant were two of the early great songwriters to migrate
to Nashville. They showed a lot of people the way. Many of their songs, recorded
by the Everly Brothers, greatly influenced the Beatles, who, in turn, influenced
the whole world of music. The Bryants changed the direction of music all over the
world through their songs for the Everly Brothers."

– CHET ATKINS

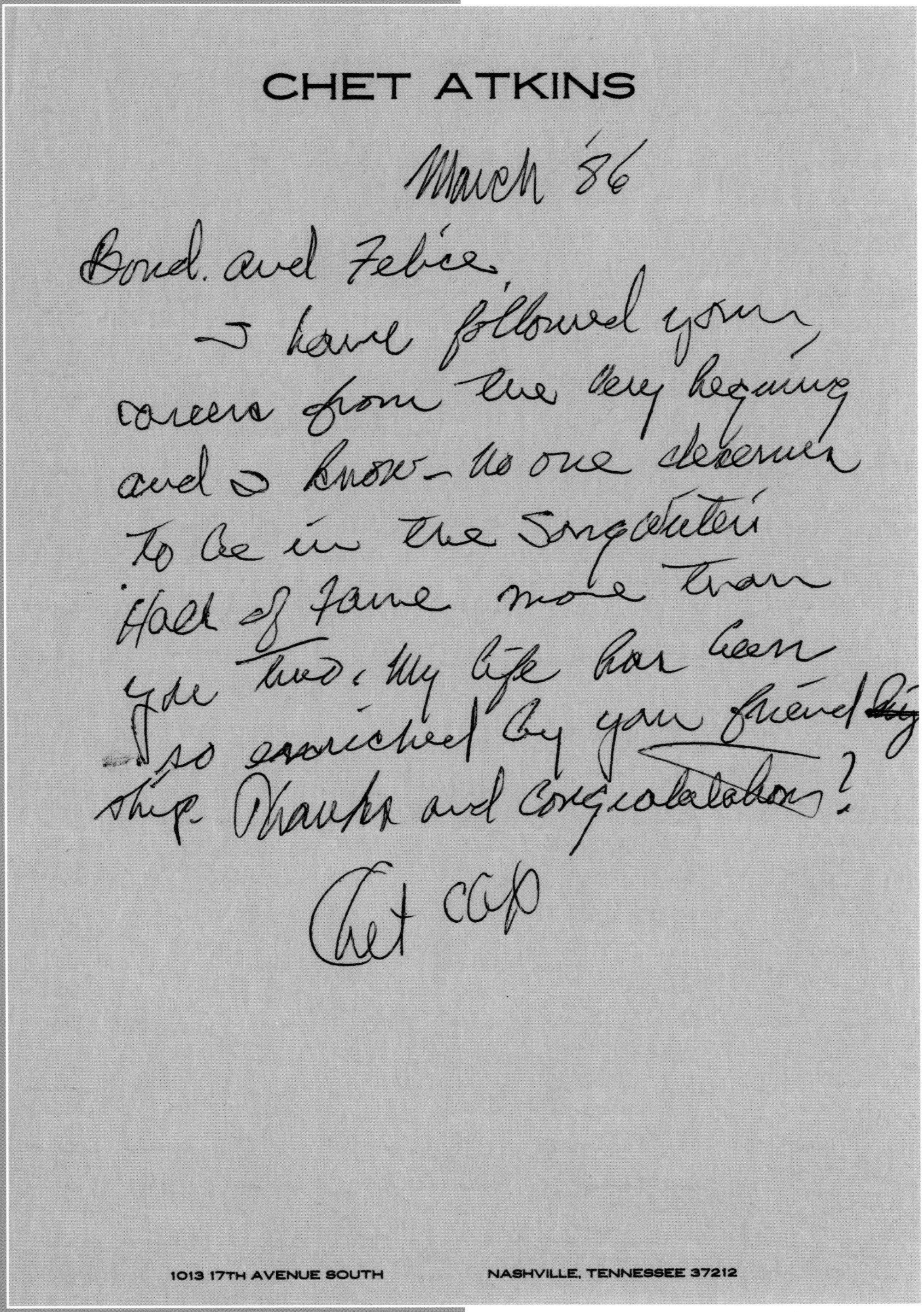

CHET ATKINS

March '86

Boud. and Felice,

I have followed your careers from the very begining and I know – no one deserves to be in the Songwriters Hall of fame more than you two. My life has been so enriched by your friendship. Thanks and congratulations!

Chet

1013 17TH AVENUE SOUTH   NASHVILLE, TENNESSEE 37212

Note to the Bryants from Chet Atkins, congratulating them on their induction into the national Songwriters Hall of Fame

Dear Boudleaux and Felice,

With love I recall,
I remember it all
like it was yesterday.
You wrote such songs,
they were so strong
they took us all the way
That's the best of my memories
and they'll always be

for we were the arrows
and you were the bow,
it took your strength
to make us go

your aim was so true
that's how I know
we were just arrows
but you were the bow

Love
Phil

Phil Everly of the Everly Brothers wrote this
poem in tribute to the Bryants.

Phil Everly and Felice Bryant, Gatlinburg, Tennessee, c. 1990

Boudleaux and Felice Bryant were elected to the Nashville Songwriters Hall of Fame in 1972, two years after it was founded. In 1986, the National Academy of Popular Music inducted them into its Songwriters Hall of Fame, where they joined such musical giants as Stephen Foster, Jerome Kern, and Cole Porter. In 1991, they received country music's highest honor: election to the Country Music Hall of Fame.

Still, some fans consider the Bryants' lifelong romance to be their most inspiring achievement. Married in September 1945, they stayed together until Boudleaux's death in 1987. Their love story, their songs, and their journey to the top of their profession provide a rich and enduring bounty for generations to come.

Felice Bryant wore this chiffon gown, embellished with beads, at the CMA Awards in 1991, when she and Boudleaux were inducted into the Country Music Hall of Fame.

Boudleaux and Felice Bryant
Rocky Top Tennessee, U.S.A.

March 21, 1986

Dear Friends.

When I learned that you had been inducted into the National Songwriter's Hall of Fame I was elated! My only question; 'what took them so long?'. I love your songs almost as much as I love you. And Boy, that's saying something!!

You know come to think of it, I couldn't be more happy, if someone in my own family had received this great honor. But, as you know, I've always considered you family any way - Whether you claim me or not.

By the way, could I possibly have a picture of the actual award?? After all, didn't I remember your lyrics and interpret your demos for years?? Boudleaux, you've probably forgotten enough songs to be installed Twice!

Give my Love to felice and my warmest congratulations to you both. No one deserves it more ...

Always,
Fred

Fred Foster
Nashville, Tn.

Congratulatory letter to the Bryants from producer, songwriter, and music executive Fred Foster, 1986

From left: Boudleaux Bryant, Wesley Rose, Roy Orbison, and Fred Foster (seated), mid-1960s

Country singer Eddy Arnold with the Rolling Stones' Keith Richards and
Charlie Watts (seated), 1965. *Photo: Michael Ochs Archives/Getty Images*

My Dear
Felice,
I'm not a big one
for fan letters,
you get one
from me.
Always,
Devoted
to you
Love Keith.

P.S. I've got a ballad
or two.
How about it?

My Dear
Felice,

I realize that
the previous
FAX had
no I.D. on it.

House of Richards.
(It's the best I could do).
KEITH RICHARDS
FAX # 203:226 6897.

Fan letter to Felice Bryant from Rolling
Stones guitarist Keith Richards

95

The Bryants with Roy Clark on *Hee Haw* in 1982. The couple wrote "Come Live with Me," Roy Clark's first #1 hit (1973).

SONGS BY BOUDLEAUX AND FELICE BRYANT

These songs, with the names of some artists who have recorded them, demonstrate the breadth and depth of the Bryants' artistic and commercial success as professional songwriters. As of 2019, approximately nine hundred different acts have recorded Bryant-written songs, selling 500 million recordings worldwide. In addition, millions of individuals have enjoyed these artists and songs on radio and television, in commercials, movies, and streamed performances.

All I Have to Do Is Dream
Paul Anka
Eddy Arnold
Richard Chamberlain
Rosemary Clooney
The Ray Conniff Singers
Rosie Flores and Ray Campi
Bobbie Gentry and Glen Campbell
Andy Gibb and Victoria Principal
Jan and Dean
The Lettermen
Linda Ronstadt
Barry Manilow
Johnny Nash
The Nitty Gritty Dirt Band
Roy Orbison
Johnny Ray
Cliff Richard and Olivia Newton-John
David Schnaufer
Billie Jo Spears
Roger Whittaker

Bird Dog
The Bellamy Brothers
The Everly Brothers

The Greg Austin Band
Joan Jett and the Blackhearts
Carl Perkins

Bye Bye Love
The Count Basie Orchestra
Ray Charles
Rita Coolidge
Lacy J. Dalton
The Everly Brothers
Connie Francis
Grateful Dead with Joan Baez
George Harrison
Shirley Horn
Brian Hyland
The Kendalls
The Anita Kerr Singers
Trini Lopez
Loretta Lynn and Conway Twitty
Moe Bandy and Joe Stampley
Anne Murray
The Newbeats
Daniel O'Donnell
Roy Orbison
Tony Orlando
Donny Osmond

Webb Pierce
The Platters
The Pozo-Seco Singers
Simon & Garfunkel
Della Reese
The Righteous Brothers
The Tokyo Union Big Band
Tompall and the Glaser Brothers
Ben Vereen & Roy Scheider
Billy Walker

Christmas Can't Be Far Away
Eddy Arnold
Burl Ives

Come Live with Me
Ray Charles
Roy Clark
Hank Snow

Country Gentleman
Chet Atkins
Chet Atkins and the Boston
   Pops Orchestra
Floyd Cramer

Buddy Holly

Nazareth

Danny Davis and the
   Nashville Brass
Albert Lee

Country Boy
Little Jimmy Dickens

Devoted to You
The Beach Boys
The Everly Brothers
Linda Ronstadt
Carly Simon and James Taylor

Have a Good Time
Tony Bennett with Percy Faith
   and His Orchestra
Ruth Brown with the James
   Quintet and Orchestra
Hank Crawford and the Marty
   Paich Orchestra

Billy Eckstine
Roy Hamilton
The Gordon Jenkins Orchestra
Sue Thompson
Joe Williams, with Harry "Sweets"
   Edison and His Orchestra

Hey, Joe!
Moe Bandy and Joe Stampley
   (as "Hey, Joe! Hey, Moe!")
Cab Calloway with the Four Bells
Goldie Hill
Frank Ifield
Frankie Laine
Bob Luman
Chuck Mead and His Grassy
   Knoll Boys with Bobby Bare
The Searchers
Carl Smith
Kitty Wells

How's the World Treating You
Eddy Arnold
Mandy Barnett
Rosemary Clooney
Johnny Duncan
Red Foley
Connie Francis
Billy Grammer
Joey + Rory
Goldie Hill
Chris Isaak
Sonny James
Alison Krauss and James Taylor
The Louvin Brothers
Elvis Presley
Jim Reeves
Sarah Vaughan
Dottie West and Don Gibson

I Can Hear Kentucky Calling Me

Boudleaux and Felice Bryant

The Osborne Brothers

It's a Lovely, Lovely World

Gail Davies

Carl Smith

Love Hurts

Bonnie Bramlett and Mr. Groove Band

Pat Boone

Jim Capaldi

Cher

Lacy J. Dalton

The Everly Brothers

Emmylou Harris

Joan Jett

Little Milton with Lucinda Williams

Don McLean

Nazareth

Sinéad O'Connor

Roy Orbison

Gram Parsons

Rod Stewart

Jimmy Webb

Mexico

Herb Alpert and the Tijuana Brass

The Bill Black Combo

The Bob Moore Orchestra

Billy Vaughn

The Ventures

Out Behind the Barn

Little Jimmy Dickens

Hardrock Gunter

Bobby Lord

The Osborne Brothers

Little Ronnie Reno

Poor Jenny

The Everly Brothers

Raining in My Heart

Connie Francis

Buddy Holly

Wanda Jackson

Dean Martin

Hank Marvin

Anne Murray

Ray Price

Tommy Roe

Leo Sayer

Status Quo

James Taylor and Carly Simon

Rocky Top

Bill Anderson

Lynn Anderson

Chet Atkins

Ace Cannon and Al Hirt

Mother Maybelle Carter

Roy Clark

Vassar Clements

Dick Curless

Skeeter Davis

Jimmy Dean

Dave Dudley

The Everly Brothers

Glenda Faye

The Flying Burrito Brothers

Rose Maddox with the
  Vern Williams Band

Charlie McCoy

Mr. Jack Daniel's Original
  Silver Cornet Band

The Nashville Symphony Orchestra

The Nitty Gritty Dirt Band

The Osborne Brothers

Buck Owens

Dolly Parton

Boots Randolph

Dinah Shore

Billie Jo Spears

John Stewart

Conway Twitty

Porter Wagoner

Joey Welz

Dottie West

Roger Whittaker

Otis Williams and the
  Midnight Cowboys

The Wood Brothers

Glenn Yarbrough

She Wears My Ring

Jimmy Bell

Roy Orbison

Elvis Presley

Ray Price

Hank Snow

Sleepless Nights

Beck and Norah Jones

Elvis Costello

The Everly Brothers

Robbie Fulks and Brennen Leigh

Emmylou Harris

Norah Jones

The Judds

Albert Lee and Hogan's Heroes

Patty Loveless featuring Vince Gill

Gram Parsons with Emmylou Harris

Pearl Jam

Peter and Gordon

Lucinda Williams

Take a Message to Mary

Jackie Brown

Don Cherry

Bob Dylan

Jack Eubanks and the Sound
  of the South

The Everly Brothers

Nick Lowe and Dave Edmunds

Kat Onoma

Ken Parker

Paul Rich

Teddy Thompson featuring
  Linda Thompson

Wake Up Little Susie

Mike Berry

The Everly Brothers

The Flying Burrito Brothers

Frankie Lymon and the Teenagers

The Grateful Dead

Loggins and Messina

Osmar Milani e sua Orquestra

The Shadows

Simon & Garfunkel

Leroy Van Dyke

Joey Welz

We Could

Ray Charles

Little Jimmy Dickens

Al Martino

Charley Pride

Learn More About the Bryants

Insider Lee Wilson, daughter-in-law to the Bryants through her marriage to their son Dane, has assembled the most comprehensive package of Bryant materials available to date. Comprising three CDs, a DVD, and an accompanying book, *All I Have to Do Is Dream: The Boudleaux and Felice Bryant Story* was released in 2011 by House of Bryant Publications. Wilson published the book by itself, under the same title, in 2017, through Two Creeks Press. Though neither can be found readily in book and record stores, they do seem to be available from Amazon.

Bill C. Malone, author of the classic country music text *Country Music USA*, and his wife, Bobbie Malone, collaborated on the forthcoming volume *Nashville's Songwriting Sweethearts: The Boudleaux and Felice Bryant Story*, published by the University of Oklahoma Press. The book will appear in 2020. The 2019 documentary film series by Ken Burns, titled *Country Music*, includes important information about the Bryants.

Because they made their living writing songs, the Bryants aimed to compose hits that would get radio airplay and become embedded in the performing repertoires of the artists who recorded their songs. Reaching the public's ears (and hearts) meant greater income. To appreciate and understand the Bryants' art, it should be experienced one hit at a time. Here are the titles of some of the couple's songwriting triumphs, followed by names of artists who had special success with those songs:

"All I Have to Do Is Dream" – Everly Brothers
"Bird Dog" – Everly Brothers
"Blue Boy" – Jim Reeves
"Bye Bye Love" – Ray Charles
"Bye Bye Love" – Everly Brothers
"Country Boy" – Little Jimmy Dickens
"Country Gentleman" – Chet Atkins
"Devoted to You" – Everly Brothers
"Devoted to You" – Carly Simon and James Taylor
"Have a Good Time" – Ruth Brown
"Hey, Joe!" – Carl Smith
"Hey, Joe!" – Frankie Laine
"How's the World Treating You" – Louvin Brothers
"How's the World Treating You" – Alison Krauss/James Taylor
"Let's Think About Living" – Bob Luman
"Like Strangers" – Emmylou Harris
"Love Hurts" – Nazareth
"Midnight" – Red Foley
"Raining in My Heart" – Buddy Holly
"Rocky Top" – Osborne Brothers
"She Wears My Ring" – Jimmy Bell (Jimmy Sweeney)
"Sleepless Nights" – Patty Loveless and Vince Gill
"Sleepless Nights" – Eddie Vedder
"Take a Message to Mary" – Bob Dylan
"Wake Up Little Susie" – Everly Brothers
"We Could" – John Prine and Iris DeMent

Other recording collections include:

Boudleaux and Felice Bryant, *Demos from the House of Bryant* (House of Bryant, 2011)

Felice and Boudleaux Bryant, *A Touch of Bryant* (CMH, 1980)

Standards from the House of Bryant (House of Bryant, 1990)

I'M ALRIGHT LYNN ANDERSON

I'M ALRIGHT • ROCKY TOP • HAUNTED HOUSE • DOWN IN THE BOONDOCKS
TRY A LITTLE KINDNESS • LOVE ME, LOVE ME • SEVEN LONELY DAYS
MY FRIEND • IF THE CREEKS DON'T RISE • THE PILLOW THAT WHISPERS

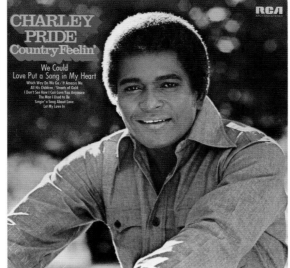

RCA

CHARLEY PRIDE
Country Feelin'

We Could
Love Put a Song in My Heart
Which Way Do We Go / It Amazes Me
All His Children / Streets of Gold
I Don't See How I Can Love You Anymore
The Man I Used to Be
Singin' a Song About Love
Let My Love In

TENDER TUNES
RCA VICTOR
A "New Orthophonic" High Fidelity Recording

THE
INTIMATE
JIM
REEVES

LPM-2216

LOVE HURTS DOWN
NAZARETH

S 53639
STEREO

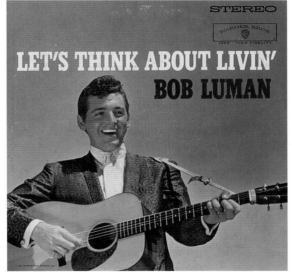

STEREO

WARNER BROS.
1996 High Fidelity

LET'S THINK ABOUT LIVIN'
BOB LUMAN

DL 75094   STEREO

COUNTRY FEELIN'
DINAH SHORE

LITTLE GREEN APPLES   MAKE THE WORLD GO AWAY
ROCKY TOP   CRYING TIME
EVIL ON MY MIND   BACK IN THE RACE
TEAR TIME   WITH PEN IN HAND
I'M LIVING IN TWO WORLDS   BABY
HE CALLED ME BABY

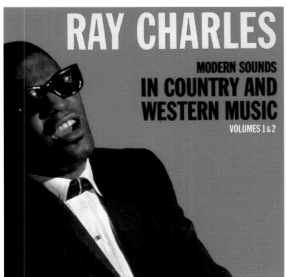

RAY CHARLES
MODERN SOUNDS
IN COUNTRY AND
WESTERN MUSIC
VOLUMES 1 & 2

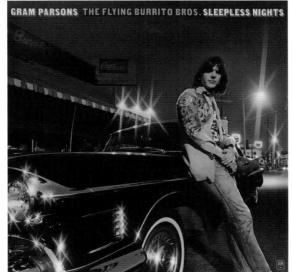

GRAM PARSONS   THE FLYING BURRITO BROS.   SLEEPLESS NIGHTS

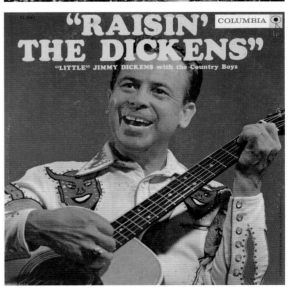

COLUMBIA

"RAISIN'
THE DICKENS"
"LITTLE" JIMMY DICKENS with the Country Boys

DL 8042

CADENCE

Acuff-Rose
MI
Time: 1:54
355

Vocal With
Orchestra
HB-403
J09W-0167
45 RPM

PROBLEMS
F. Bryant B. Bryant
THE EVERLY BROTHERS

CADENCE RECORDS INC. NEW YORK, N.Y.

GRAM PARSONS
and the FALLEN ANGELS
Produced by John Delgatto & Marley Brant

Sierra
Records

45 RPM
PROMOTIONAL
NOT FOR SALE
45-105A

Intro. :12

LOVE HURTS
(Boudleaux Bryant)
℗ 1982 Warner Bros. Records, Inc.
© 1982 Sierra Records
From the Sierra Records LP
GRAM PARSONS
AND THE FALLEN ANGELS
LIVE 1973 GP 1973
Pasadena, CA. 91107-0853 • Made in USA

House of Bryant
Publ., BMI

4:34

MFG. BY SIERRA RECORDS • ALL RIGHTS RESERVED

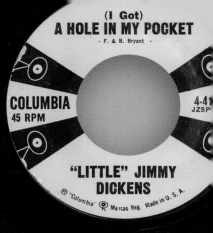

(I Got)
A HOLE IN MY POCKET
- F. & B. Bryant -

COLUMBIA
45 RPM

4-41
JZSP

"LITTLE" JIMMY
DICKENS

® "Columbia" ⓜ Marcas Reg. Made in U. S. A.

CMH
PROMO/NOT FOR SALE

STEREO

℗ 1980
CMH Records, Inc.
All Rights
Reserved

FELICE &
BOUDLEAUX

CMH-1539
(CMH-6147-S)
2:28
(Intro :12)
Produced by
Steve Singleton
From the album
"A Touch of
Bryant"
CMH-6243

I CAN HEAR KENTUCKY CALLING ME
(B. & F. Bryant)
House of Bryant Publications (BMI)

CMH RECORDS, INC. • P.O. BOX 39439 • LOS ANGELES, CA 90039

Monument

MO 652
Pub. Acuff - Rose
Publ. - BMI

45-438
Time 2:26

LOVE HURTS
(B. Bryant)
ROY ORBISON
with Bob Moore's Orch.
& Chorus

LET'S THINK
ABOUT LIVING
(Boudleaux Bryant)

WB
RECORDS

Acuff-Rose Pe
BMI
2:03
5172
(C11503)

BOB LUMAN

COLUMBIA

45 RPM
4-21437
(ZSP36591)

HAWK-EYE
-Boudleaux Bryant-
BOBBY LORD

Trade Marks ® ⓜ Marcas and ⓜ Made in U.S.A.

DECCA

Reg. U.S. Pat. Off. Marcas Registrada Mfrd by Decca Records

32864
(122,893)
(2:21)

A

PROMOTION
COPY
NOT FOR SALE

House Of Bryant
Publ. (BMI)

MUDDY BOTTOM
(Boudleaux Bryant-Felice Bryant)
THE OSBORNE BROTHERS

CMH
PROMO/NOT FOR SALE

STEREO

℗ 1980
CMH Record
All Rights
Reserved

FELICE &
BOUDLEAUX
Produced by
Steve Singleton
From th
"A To
Bry
CMH-

CMH-
(CMH-6
2:
(Intro

KEEPIN' WARM
(B. & F. Bryant)
House of Bryant Publications (BMI)

CMH RECORDS, IN
ANGELES, CA

Sources

Interviews

Available on the Internet:

Bart, Teddy. Interview with Boudleaux and Felice Bryant, *Teddy Bart Show*, 1983. Available at YouTube.

Bryant, Felice. Interview for the Grammy Foundation Living History Interview Series. Available at YouTube.

Campbell, Archie. Interview with Boudleaux and Felice Bryant, *Yesteryear in Nashville*, 1983. Available at YouTube.

Frist Library and Archive, Country Music Hall of Fame and Museum, Nashville, TN:

Hall, Patricia A. Interview with Boudleaux and Felice Bryant, Nashville, TN, November 19, 1975.

Representative of Broadcast Music, Inc. Interview with Wesley Rose, 1984, for BMI archives.

Rumble, John. Interview with Boudleaux and Felice Bryant, Gatlinburg, TN, March 26, 1983.

Rumble, John. Interview with Boudleaux and Felice Bryant, Nashville, TN, May 12, 1983.

Rumble, John. Interview with Fred Foster, Nashville, TN, November 15, 2000.

Audio and Video Recordings

All I Have to Do Is Dream: The Boudleaux and Felice Bryant Story. Notes by Lee Wilson. Three CDs. One DVD. Nashville, TN: House of Bryant, 2011.

Burns, Ken. *Country Music*, 2019.

Everly Brothers, *Classic Everly Brothers*. Notes by Colin Escott. Three CDs. Bear Family Records, 1992.

Various Artists, *Boudleaux and Felice, Volume II: The Early Years*. Notes by Paul Kingsbury. Two CDs. Gatlinburg, TN: House of Bryant Publications, 1991.

Various Artists, *Standards from the House of Bryant*. One CD. Gatlinburg, TN: House of Bryant, 1990.

Books

Encyclopedia of Country Music: The Ultimate Guide to the Music. Edited by Paul Kingsbury, Michael McCall, and John W. Rumble. Second Edition. New York: Oxford University Press, 2012.

Horstman, Dorothy. *Sing Your Heart Out, Country Boy: Classic Country Songs and Their Inside Stories by the Men and Women Who Wrote Them*. Nashville: Country Music Foundation Press, 1996.

Karpp, Phyllis. *Ike's Boys: The Story of the Everly Brothers*. Ann Arbor, MI: Pierian Press, 1988.

White, Roger. *The Everly Brothers: Walk Right Back*. London: Plexus, 1994.

Periodicals

Hutchinson, Lydia. "Boudleaux and Felice Bryant." PerformingSongwriter.com, January 14, 2015.

Loder, Kurt. "The Everly Brothers: The *Rolling Stone* Interview." *Rolling Stone*, May 8, 1986.

Thanki, Juli. "'Rocky Top' at 50: How a Throw-in Tune Became Tennessee's Most Beloved Anthem," *The Tennessean*, September 3, 2017.

CIRCLE GUARD

The Country Music Hall of Fame and Museum Circle Guard unites and celebrates individuals who have given their time, talent, and treasure to safeguard the integrity of country music and make it accessible to a global audience through the Museum. The Circle Guard designation ranks as the grandest distinction afforded to those whose unwavering commitment to the Museum protects the legacies of the members of the Country Music Hall of Fame, and, by extension, the time-honored achievements of all who are part of the country music story.

INAUGURAL CLASS

Steve Turner, Founder

Kyle Young, Commander General

David Conrad

J. William Denny

Mary Ann McCready

Seab Tuck

Felice and Boudleaux Bryant, *Music City News*, 1980